Standards-Based Connections
Reading
Grade 4

Carson-Dellosa Publishing, LLC
Greensboro, North Carolina

Credits
Content Editor: Bitsy Griffin
Copy Editor: Christine M. Schwab

Visit *carsondellosa.com* for correlations to Common Core, state, national, and Canadian provincial standards.

Carson-Dellosa Publishing, LLC
PO Box 35665
Greensboro, NC 27425 USA
carsondellosa.com

ISBN 978-1-4838-2477-2

01-188151151

Table of Contents

Introduction

Reading comprehension is an essential skill for enabling school, college, and career success. This book focuses on five reading comprehension skills: story elements, summarizing, compare and contrast, cause and effect, and inferring. Emphasized are the reading standards in the Common Core State Standards.

The reading standards set expectations for each grade level and define what students should understand and be able to do. They are designed to be more rigorous and allow for students to justify their thinking. They reflect the knowledge that is necessary for success in college and career readiness. Students who master the standards as they advance through the grades exhibit the following capabilities:

1. They demonstrate independence.
2. They build strong content knowledge.
3. They respond to the varying demands of audience, task, purpose, and discipline.
4. They comprehend as well as critique.
5. They value evidence.
6. They use technology and digital media strategically and capably.
7. They come to understand other perspectives and cultures.*

How to Use This Book

This book is a collection of grade-appropriate practice pages aligned to the reading sections of the Common Core State Standards for English Language Arts. Included is an alignment matrix to show exactly which standards are addressed on the practice pages. Also included are a skill assessment and a skill assessment analysis. Use the assessment at the beginning of the year or at any time you wish to assess your students' mastery of certain standards. The analysis connects each test item to a practice page or set of practice pages so that you can review skills with students who struggle in certain areas.

*© Copyright 2010 National Governors Association Center for Best Practices and Council of Chief State School Officers. All rights reserved.

Common Core State Standards Alignment Matrix

Page #	12	13	14	15	16	17	18	19	20	21	22	23	24	25	26	27	28	29	30	31	32	33	34	35	36	37	38	39	40	41	42	43	44	45	46	47	48	49	50	51
4.RL.1																															•									
4.RL.2																			•	•	•	•				•		•		•	•									
4.RL.3			•	•	•	•	•	•	•	•		•	•	•								•																•		
4.RL.4																					•																			
4.RL.5	•	•	•																																					•
4.RL.6												•																		•										•
4.RL.7																										•														
4.RL.8																																								
4.RL.9																																	•	•	•					
4.RL.10		•	•			•				•	•	•	•	•	•	•			•		•	•							•			•				•		•		•
4.RI.1																								•	•															
4.RI.2																	•							•		•		•	•											
4.RI.3																																								
4.RI.4																		•																		•	•		•	
4.RI.5																									•				•											
4.RI.6																																								
4.RI.7																•								•																
4.RI.8																									•															
4.RI.9																•		•											•							•		•		
4.RI.10																•	•						•	•	•	•		•												

Page #	52	53	54	55	56	57	58	59	60	61	62	63	64	65	66	67	68	69	70	71	72	73	74	75	76	77	78	79	80	81	82	83	84	85	86	87	88	89	90	91
4.RL.1										•									•	•			•		•	•	•			•	•		•			•	•		•	•
4.RL.2																						•		•						•									•	
4.RL.3		•									•	•	•	•																										
4.RL.4																												•												
4.RL.5																																								
4.RL.6																																								
4.RL.7											•	•															•				•		•		•					
4.RL.8																																								
4.RL.9			•		•				•																															
4.RL.10	•	•					•					•			•				•				•	•	•			•	•		•		•			•	•	•		•
4.RI.1																																		•						
4.RI.2																																								
4.RI.3					•			•										•			•																			
4.RI.4																																		•						
4.RI.5															•																									
4.RI.6																																								
4.RI.7			•						•																															
4.RI.8								•																																
4.RI.9					•																																			
4.RI.10					•		•										•	•			•																			

© Carson-Dellosa • CD-104661

Name_____

Read the story. Answer the questions.

The Persuasive Paper

India thought about her assignment. She had not written a persuasive paper before. Now, she had to come up with an important topic. Her friend Miguel was thinking about cafeteria food. Lola was going to write about adoption. Finally, India decided to write about recess.

India created a two-part survey asking:

1. Should students have more or less recess?

2. Why?

India talked with all of the students in her class. Next, she talked with some neighbors. She decided to argue for more recess. Now, she had to decide on three reasons to support more recess.

Reading the survey results, India saw her classmates had one preferred answer. They wanted more recess because it was fun! Other reasons were:

- Sunlight is healthier than indoor light.

- Exercise helps your brain work better.

- Everyone needs a break from work.

- Recess helps students learn how to get along.

Choosing the three best reasons would be hard. She could use the most popular reason, but that might not be the best for her paper. India decided she needed to do some more reading about recess to help her choose the most important reason.

1. What genre is this story? Circle the correct answer.

    fantasy   realistic fiction   historical fiction   science fiction

2. What is the problem that India has to solve?

_____

_____

3. Summarize in a sentence or two what India does to prepare for her paper.

_____

_____

4. How did talking with others help India decide to write her paper in favor of more recess at school? _____

_____

5. Circle the definition that best explains the meaning of the word *persuasive*.

   a. Convincing someone to support your idea.

   b. Presenting your idea in a positive way.

   c. Learning more about a topic.

6. What is one reason from the survey results that would help India most effectively make her case for more recess? Why do you think this is the strongest reason? _____

_____

7. Circle the best title for India's paper.

   a. Recess Is Fun   b. A Case for More Recess   c. Recess: A Persuasive Paper

8. India made a pie chart to show the survey results. Do you think this is a good choice for her visual? _____

   Why or why not? _____

_____

9. Do you think India's message would be as strong if she were to write a poem? _____

_____

   Why or why not? _____

_____

10. How might a principal's thoughts on extra recess be different than India's ideas? How would they be the same? Write your ideas in the table.

Same	Different

11. How did India's work affect her paper? _____

   What reasons from the story make you think that? _____

_____

Read the passage. Answer the questions.

Mount St. Helens

Mount St. Helens is a volcano. It sits in the southwest part of Washington state. In 1857, the volcano erupted. Magma and waste spread across the land. After that, the volcano sat quietly for over 100 years. Scientists built a watch post nearby. They observed the volcano carefully. They looked for changes.

In March 1980, Mount St. Helens changed. The sleeping volcano woke up. On March 16, people felt small earthquakes. In a few days, the earthquakes became stronger.

The volcano looked different too. Hot gases formed inside the volcano. They pushed part of the ground out into a bulge. On March 27, people heard an explosion. The volcano coughed steam and ash.

May 18 was a Sunday morning. Another earthquake shook the mountain. Part of the mountain broke off. The volcano erupted. Hot gases and ash flew 16 miles (25.75 km) into the sky. Melted ice and parts of the earth formed a **lahar**, a kind of mudflow or debris flow. The lahar covered 17 miles (27.36 km). Ash was seen over 900 miles (1,448.41 km) away. The area became a national park in 1982.

12. What is the setting of this passage? _____

13. Circle the sentence that best gives the main idea of the text.

   a. Volcanoes are dangerous.

   b. Volcanoes can sit for a long time.

   c. Volcanoes give signals that they are about to erupt.

14. What specific information helped you choose the main idea?

   _____

   _____

15. What words did the author use that made the volcano seem alive?

   _____

   _____

16. Circle the best description of how this passage is structured.

   a. Compare and contrast

   b. Sequence of events

   c. Problem and solution

17.   What are three significant events leading up to this volcanic eruption?

_____

_____

_____

18.   What other stories have you read about volcanoes? _____

How are these stories similar to this event?

_____

_____

19.   Circle the correct answer. Using clues found in the text, *lahar* means

a. landslide.   b. lava flow.   c. eruption.

20.   Draw a time line to show the events of the 1980 eruption of Mount St. Helens.

21.   What do you think the people in the area were thinking and feeling as the events on your time line were happening?

_____

_____

22.   Do you think the scientists watching the volcano felt the same way as tourists did?

_____

How might they feel the same or differently?

_____

_____

23.   Why do you think Mount St. Helens was chosen to become a national park?

_____

_____

24.   Think about a print resource for reading more about the 1980 eruption of Mount St. Helens. What might the title be?

_____

Read the passage. Answer the questions.

The Dewey Decimal System

Most school libraries look similar. Books are arranged in a certain way. Why is this important? It means you can find a book in a precise place. Books are organized by their subjects. If you know what the book is about, it is easy to find. Do you need a book on the environment? Look in the 300s. Do you want to look up facts on animals? The 500 section is the place to be. Do you need a cookbook? Skip over to the 600s. You can find the books you need if you know a few rules.

Books were not always organized this way. Each library arranged books differently. One library might order books by purchase date. Another library might have all the green books together. Another could alphabetize all of the books by title. This must have been very confusing for visitors.

In the late 1800s, Melvil Dewey was a librarian. He wanted to reorganize libraries. He wanted to reorganize them all the same way. Mr. Dewey came up with 10 major divisions for books. Each major division is also divided into sections. The 10 major divisions are listed below:

000 – General works   500 – Sciences

100 – Psychology   600 – Technology

200 – Religion   700 – Arts and Recreation

300 – Social Sciences   800 – Literature

400 – Language   900 – Geography and History

This is how most school libraries are set up. Mr. Dewey's work means you can find the same book in the same place in most libraries.

25. What problem did Dewey want to solve?

_____

_____

26. What was his solution?

_____

_____

27. How do you think librarians at the time felt about Dewey's reorganization ideas?

_____

_____

28. Read each pair of sentences. Write **C** on the line by the cause. Write **E** on the line by the effect.

   a. Libraries were all arranged differently. _____

      Dewey thought of a new library organization. _____

   b. Sports are in the 700 section. _____

      The 700 section is about arts and recreation. _____

   c. Every green book is on one shelf. _____

      Chloe cannot find the book on mice. _____

29. Mr. Lewis is thinking about organizing his elementary library like a bookstore. Write a letter of advice to him from Mr. Dewey. Include reasons from the story in your letter.

   _____

   _____

   _____

   _____

   _____

   _____

   _____

   _____

30. Read and identify each sentence as either fact or opinion. Circle your answer.

   a. Melvil Dewey was a librarian.   fact   opinion

   b. Other librarians did not like Dewey.   fact   opinion

   c. Putting books in the 400 section is silly.   fact   opinion

   d. Many libraries are organized by the Dewey decimal system.   fact   opinion

After you score each student's skill assessment pages, match any incorrectly answered problems to the table below. Use the corresponding practice pages for any problem areas, and ensure that each student receives remediation in these areas.

1. realistic fiction; 2. what to write the paper about; 3. Answers will vary but may include that India thinks about topics, and she decides on recess. She gives friends and neighbors a survey. 4. Answers will vary. 5. a; 6. Answers will vary. 7. b; 8. Answers will vary. 9. Answers will vary. 10. Answers will vary but may include: Same—need for more recess, good to get away from the classroom; Different—Principal thinks students need more time for study. India thinks students may be more willing to study at home. 11. Answers will vary. 12. Mount St. Helens, Washington; 13. c. Volcanoes give signals that they are about to erupt. 14. Answers will vary. 15. sleeping, woke up, coughed; 16. b. Sequence of events; 17. earthquakes, bulge formed, explosion of steam and gas; 18. Answers will vary. 19. a. landslide. 20. Check that time lines contain significant events. 21. Answers will vary. 22. Answers will vary. 23. the volcanic eruption; 24. Answers will vary. 25. Libraries were all organized differently. 26. He came up with 10 major categories for the subjects of books. 27. Answers will vary but may include: Some may have been excited about the guidelines. 28. a. c, e; b. e, c; c. c, c; 29. Answers will vary. 30. a. fact; b. opinion; c. opinion; d. fact

Comprehension Skill	Common Core State Standards*	Assessment Item(s)	Practice Page(s)
Reading Standards for Literature			
Story Elements	4.RL.3, 4.RL.5	1, 2, 9	12–27
Summarizing	4.RL.2, 4.RL.7	3, 7, 8	30–33, 38, 40, 42, 43
Compare and Contrast	4.RL.6, 4.RL.9	10,	44–55, 57
Cause and Effect	4.RL.1	4, 6, 11	60–67, 71, 73–75
Inferring	4.RL.1, 4.RL.4	4, 5	76–84, 86–91
Reading Standards for Informational Text			
Story Elements	4.RI.3, 4.RI.5	12, 16, 17, 25, 26	
Summarizing	4.RI.2, 4.RI.7	13, 14, 17, 20, 26	28, 29, 34–37, 39, 41
Compare and Contrast	4.RI.6, 4.RI.9	18, 22, 24, 27, 29, 30	56, 58, 59
Cause and Effect	4.RI.1, 4.RI.8	21, 23, 27, 28	68–70, 72
Inferring	4.RI.1, 4.RI.4	15, 19, 21, 27	85

* © Copyright 2010 National Governors Association Center for Best Practices and Council of Chief State School Officers. All rights reserved.

"Write" Now

Circle the correct genre to complete each sentence. Then, write the genre next to each title on the list.

1. A story set on another planet would probably be _____ .

   science fiction   biography   historical fiction

2. A book of haiku written in the fifteenth century would be _____ .

   drama   poetry   adventure

3. A book set in New Orleans during the American Civil War most likely would

   be _____ .

   fairy tale   fantasy   historical fiction

4. A book about the life of Martin Luther King Jr. would be a _____ .

   poetry   biography   mystery

5. A book with talking animals as characters probably would

   be a_____ .

   biography   mystery   folktale

6. *Cinderella* _____

7. *Middle School on Mars* _____

8. *The Life of Sitting Bull* _____

9. *The Knight and the Dragon* _____

10. *Rhymes for All Seasons* _____

☐   I can use proper terms to explain the differences between poems, drama, and prose.

Different Kinds of Stories

Read each paragraph. Circle the correct genre.

1. I hopped on the magnet van after my group meeting at the Eduplex. We had met to discuss research for our paper entitled "Foods Across the Galaxies." We could have met by hologram, but our mentor, Sean Wang, suggested that we share the same space. So, now I am riding in this magnet van, zipping along 20 feet (6.1 m) above the flat surface of the Gobi Desert.

    fantasy   realistic fiction   historical fiction   science fiction

2. Grandpa held me in his arms as he stretched his wings. Lifting up into the air, he flew us over the forest. "It's OK, Petey. I won't let go." I just had to cry, so I pressed my face into Grandpa's shoulder and wept softly. We were moving to a new forest, and I hated to leave my old home behind. I could tell we were slowing down and dropping steadily. "Almost there," murmured Grandpa. We landed in front of our clan's new tree home. Grandpa folded his wings, and we went inside.

    fantasy   realistic fiction   historical fiction   science fiction

3. Pa handed me the lantern. "C'mon, Jesse," he mumbled. "The fence is broken, and we've got to fix it before any cows get loose." I hurried after him, realizing we did not have time to waste. Last year, we lost several calves, and it really hurt us. Most of the ranch hands had gone into town to unwind before next week's trail ride. So, Pa only had me for help. After he grabbed his tools, we stepped into the night air and headed for the eastern side of the fence.

    fantasy   realistic fiction   historical fiction   science fiction

4. I want nothing to do with the flower store! Mom's business was good for her . . . and good for our whole family. But, I want to work at the art gallery. Mrs. Fleming suggested that I assist her at the gallery with her Saturday morning class. Those small children are so much fun to teach! But, Mom wants me to help her on the weekends, and I do not know what to do.

    fantasy   realistic fiction   historical fiction   science fiction

☐ **I can use proper terms to explain the differences between poems, drama, and prose.**

☐ **I can read and comprehend grade-level fiction text.**

What Is It?

Read each paragraph. Choose a genre from the word bank. Write it on the line.

Word Bank				
biography	myth	realistic fiction	science fiction	tall tale

1. When Daniel Boone was a child, he came down with smallpox. According to one story, he got tired of playing outside when all of his friends were sick in bed. So, he snuck into bed with them. A few days later, Daniel got the pox. His mother was angry—and scared.

   _____

2. Our winters got so cold the lakes would freeze in minutes. That is how Lost Lake vanished. You see, a large—or rather, gigantic—flock of geese settled down upon it, and their feet froze in the water in short order. When they flew off the following morning, they took the whole lake with them.

   _____

3. Ida looked at the girl who stood in the doorway. She was Ida's clone! It was like looking into a mirror. There was no difference in face, form, coloring, or even stance. That Doctor Enselmeier! He must have perfected his clone creation project.

   _____

4. All three boys spun out on their bikes, gravel flying. School was out! Ted, in the lead as always, headed toward the park. Pumping hard, the boys sped up Hollow Hill, through the sandlot, and across the ballpark, slamming on their brakes just shy of the bleachers.

   _____

5. "Whatever you do, do not open the box, my dear." But, Pandora marveled at the box before her. It was so beautiful, what could possibly be inside? The temptation was too great to resist. Pandora was such a curious girl that she could not help lifting the lid for a quick peek. But, when she did, dark spirits suddenly flew out. They took to the skies and spread all over the world. What had she done?

   _____

6. By the time Zach was five, he had grown to six feet eight inches (2 m). His appetite was so great that his dad worked 12 hours a day just to provide Zach's meals. His voice had deepened, though he still carried a blanket and sucked his thumb. The blanket he adored was a 20-pound (9-kg) quilt that his father made for him from a 200-pound (90.7-kg) pile of old clothes.

   _____

❑ I can use proper terms to explain the differences between poems, drama, and prose.

❑ I can read and comprehend grade-level fiction text.

Who Is It?

First, match the name of each character with the most likely description. Then, create a descriptive name for each person.

_____ 1. Leo Lyons

_____ 2. Melodie Singer

_____ 3. Spuds Brown

_____ 4. Macon Potts

_____ 5. Lollie Popp

_____ 6. Ripp Kord

_____ 7. Tex Ryder

_____ 8. Stretch VanderHoop

_____ 9. Minnie Follows

_____ 10. Grace Whirling

_____ 11. Auntie Pasta

_____ 12. Willie Tripp

a. a ceramic-loving artist who sculpts pottery

b. a potato farmer from north-central Idaho

c. a four-year-old girl with sticky hands

d. a music teacher who instructs young singers

e. a stunt man known for his parachute jumps

f. a zoologist who studies African lions

g. an accident-prone boy who constantly slips and falls

h. a seven-foot (2.1 m) tall basketball star

i. a horse-loving cowhand who spends his days in the saddle

j. a petite young girl who loves to tag along with others

k. a ballerina known for her elegant pirouettes

l. an older woman who loves to cook spaghetti

13. a librarian _____

14. a train engineer _____

15. a senator _____

16. a firefighter _____

17. a golf pro _____

18. a scientist _____

☐   I can use specific details from a text to describe a character, a setting, or an event.

Stretching It

Read the sentences. They describe details from different stories. If the detail best fits a realistic story, write R on the line. If the detail best fits a fantasy story, write F on the line.

_____ 1. My dog, Petey, loves to eat ham sandwiches. He tries to swipe mine every chance he gets.

_____ 2. Lana's feet were sore. Walking two miles through the museum in one afternoon had worn holes in her sneakers.

_____ 3. Seth enjoyed hanging out with his friend Ibit. He wished he could spend more time at Ibit's house, but he was allergic to the atmosphere on Jupiter.

_____ 4. Ping could not wait until the new television arrived. He was excited about having a flat screen TV in his very own home.

_____ 5. Haley was in tears. She had lost her ticket to the concert, and the show was sold out!

_____ 6. Will was frustrated with his soccer team. They did not play as well after robots joined the league.

_____ 7. Scamper is the best pet in the world! She fetches and comes when I call her. The only problem is feeding her. It costs a lot to feed a dinosaur.

_____ 8. Quinn had a hard time walking barefoot across the hot sandy beach. As soon as she could, she dived into the water to cool off.

_____ 9. Irina made an incredible sculpture out of ice. She was sure that it would win the top prize at the arts festival.

_____ 10. Luka loved sitting in the hot tub. On a clear night, he could see one or two spaceships cross the sky.

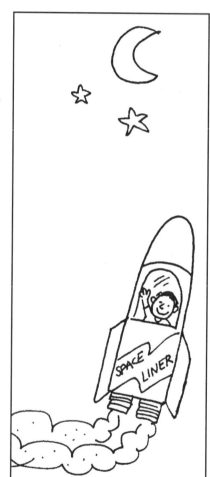

I can use specific details from a text to describe a character, a setting, or an event.

He Said, She Said

Read the lines of dialogue from different stories. Match each quote with the correct character from the list.

Character List

a. Lance Perry, an actor

b. Sharmain Steele, a registered nurse

c. Felix Brecht, a music composer

d. Bitsy Floss, a patriotic seamstress

e. Lee Deezine, a toy designer

f. Goldie Grahame, a nutritionist

g. Bill Gelbrefe, a lawyer

h. Belem El Sher, a carpet exporter

i. Robbie Hollingsworth, a teacher

j. "Lead Foot" LaRue, a truck driver

_____ 1. "Shall I administer another IV? The patient just woke up."

_____ 2. "Well, I enjoy creating toys that are fun for kids. Take this Clyde the Cat windup toy, for instance. It always lands on its feet. See?"

_____ 3. "Your daughter is a delight in my classroom. She is always the first one to raise her hand."

_____ 4. "How's my hair? Are you ready to shoot? No, I don't need a stuntman for this scene!"

_____ 5. "A healthy diet should have whole grains and lots of fresh fruits and vegetables."

_____ 6. "Hello, Jacques! Your Persian rugs are ready for shipment. I think you will be delighted when they arrive."

_____ 7. "I have almost finished sewing the flag. I am so excited for everyone to see my stars and stripes design."

_____ 8. "This traffic is making me crazy! It's slowing me down, and this delivery is late!"

_____ 9. "First, the flutes begin the melody. Then, the violins come in."

_____ 10. "Can you repeat that last statement, please? I want to make sure that everyone in the courtroom heard your testimony."

☐ **I can use specific details from a text to describe a character, a setting, or an event.**

☐ **I can read and comprehend grade-level fiction text.**

Name_____

Welcome to Our Assembly

Read lines of dialogue from a story about a school assembly. Match each quote with the correct character from the list.

Character List

a. Tony Brown: very nervous

b. Abby McMann: observant

c. Percy Pennyfeather: nosy, a busybody

d. Nadia Kovacs: arrogant, smug

e. Jodhi Amani: relieved

f. Jamal Davis: disappointed

g. Mary Marshall: serious, in charge

h. Chang Lee: hopeful, talented

_____ 1. "Quiet down, students! We have something important to discuss. I need your attention."

_____ 2. "Oh, no! Do you think they are going to announce our grades?"

_____ 3. "They are probably going to give a major award to the best student, and who else could it be but me!"

_____ 4. "I saw some teachers talking in the hall, but I couldn't overhear them."

_____ 5. "I think this is about that science award. I think I could win. My project turned out well."

_____ 6. "Look! There's that new teacher. I bet this assembly is to welcome her."

_____ 7. "Whew! I was worried they were going to cancel the school-wide festival."

_____ 8. "I thought my friend Chang was going to get that award today. Too bad!"

☐ **I can use specific details from a text to describe a character, a setting, or an event.**

18

I Have a Feeling

Read plot events from different stories. Write the name of a character to answer each question.

a. Faster than he had ever run before, Lonnie Lorenzo sped through the trees of the city park. None of the other students could catch him. Today, he was in a league of his own and was sure to win the race.

b. She swept into the brightly lit hall. This was her day! Lady Beatrice had ordered all of her lords to come to court and compete for the Golden Scepter. They had better obey!

c. Dorothy Wells stepped onto her porch and scowled at the carload of noisy, rude men parked in front of her house. She was determined to make them move before they woke the rest of the neighborhood.

d. She looked out, shivering with fear. Frank the fox had followed her to her nest. Dora, a young deer mouse, nervously pulled back into the shadows.

e. Boy, did his toe hurt! Steven hobbled over to a chair to look at his big toe. He had pretended to kick his friend Jeremy. Instead, he had kicked the wall. Steven winced as he pulled off his sock.

f. Ned Tuttle climbed into the backseat filled with excitement. Today, he was finally going to have those braces taken off of his teeth!

g. Helene stared at the diving board. It was so far above the swimming pool. Thirty years ago, when she was still a young woman, she could have easily made that dive. But now, she was not so sure. A lot of time had passed. Could she still do it?

1. Who is excited about the future? _____

2. Who seems ready for a confrontation? _____

3. Who feels good about his ability?_____

4. Who is thinking about the past?_____

5. Who seems nervous and afraid? _____

6. Who appears arrogant and determined?_____

7. Who is sorry for a mistake? _____

□   I can use specific details from a text to describe a character, a setting, or an event.

In Perspective

Match each line of dialogue with the correct time and place. Then, write a setting for each quote. Describe both the time and the place.

_____ 1. "Not much happening here. Wonder if the other side of the island is any busier."

_____ 2. "Are those animals stomping over my head? It's enough to give me a headache!"

_____ 3. "Who told Tommy to buy me a lava lamp? What a crazy gift!"

_____ 4. "Whoa! All of this swaying is making me sick."

_____ 5. "I just wanted to grab a coconut, but now I can't get down!"

a. on a treetop during a summer windstorm

b. on the shore of an island off the coast of Greenland in late autumn

c. up in a palm tree on a summer day

d. under a bridge that three goats are trying to cross

e. in the return line at a department store one afternoon

6. "I know it's a kooky style, but I think my hair looks . . . special."

_____

_____

7. "Hey, glad you finally made it to the party. Did you bring your swimsuit?"

_____

_____

8. "Ouch! What just stung me? That hurts."

_____

_____

9. "They're coming this way. Yes, I see them now. What wild costumes!"

_____

_____

10. "Honey, you shouldn't have! It's so expensive, but it really is beautiful."

_____

_____

☐ I can use specific details from a text to describe a character, a setting, or an event.

Theme Park

Read the story. Answer the questions.

"That is 17 dollars," announced Cal. He gathered all of the change spread out on his bed and placed it next to the dollar bills on the red comforter. Then, he flopped back onto the bed, making the change bounce.

"We still need 23 dollars to cover the cost of admission," frowned Cleo. "Mom said we have to have the total cost of admission before we can go to Great Mountain Theme Park." The twins sat on the bed in Cal's room, imagining the theme park. It was sure to have delicious food, great arcade games, and the best rides in the state—roller coasters, water rides, and Ferris wheels.

"It will take at least a month of allowances to have enough money," said Cal. "Besides, that would not leave any money for food or souvenirs."

"I know," Cleo said, "and I have already checked between the couch cushions, under the car seats, and in all of our jacket pockets." As the twins sat glumly, they watched colorful leaves drop from the tree outside the window.

Suddenly, an idea popped into their heads. They could rake the neighbors' leaves for cash. It was the perfect plan. Their mother would be pleased that they helped out the neighborhood, and they would get to go to the amusement park.

The twins hurried outside, grabbed two rakes from the garage, and got to work. By the end of the day, they had all the money they needed. That night, they went to sleep with dreams of the Great Mountain Theme Park floating in their heads.

1. What is the setting?

    _____

2. Who are the characters?

    _____

3. What is the problem?

    _____

4. How do they solve their problem?

    _____

☐   I can use specific details from a text to describe a character, a setting, or an event.

☐   I can read and comprehend grade-level fiction text.

Summer Camp

Read the story. Complete the activity on page 23.

Our camp is great. A bunch of kids from school go there, but I especially enjoy meeting new kids from the other schools. We sing crazy songs in the dining hall each day at noon, and there are activities and challenges to complete all day long.

This year, I got Keesha for a counselor. She is so funny! She has all of us girls rolling on the cabin floor laughing at her silly stories at bedtime. But, she is smart, too, and knows when one of us is homesick or feeling bad. She never pokes fun at us when we do something foolish, and she shows us how to express kindness to the others in our cabin.

Keesha loves nature and is studying biology at the university during the school year. She often points out the wildlife in camp. On our second day, Keesha took us on the first of many walks through the woods. At one point, she stopped and pointed to the crook of a beech tree. We saw a mother opossum with four babies on her back. They were so cute!

Once, Keesha took all 10 of us for a hike through the woods at night. She warned us to be quiet and to bring our flashlights with us. We walked for maybe 20 minutes when we stopped suddenly. We heard some chattering creatures off to our right. Down by the lake were two raccoons fighting over some bread they had found. They almost sounded like two children squabbling over a treat.

One drizzly day, she took us to a nearby national park. We took binoculars, guidebooks, insect repellent, water, and snacks. We sketched some of the wonderful flowering plants we saw. Keesha knew the history and medicinal value of many of these plants. She showed us one plant that gave off a very powerful smell when she broke it open. She told us it would keep flies and mosquitoes away. It was easy to see why that would work because the odor was horrible!

☐   **I can read and comprehend grade-level fiction text.**

Summer Camp (cont.)

Every evening after supper, we play games with campers from the other cabins. Keesha volunteered to have our cabin set up the evening game on our fifth day. We went all over the camp, setting up clues for a treasure hunt, which meant that we had to canoe to different landmarks around the lake, crawl under some of the older cabins, plan hiding spots, and race down the camp trails.

Of course, we ran out of time. When the bell rang for supper, we were still far across the field. My new friend, Rita, unknowingly stepped over a light blue-gray snake. It was huge! Keesha said it was called a blue racer. We all stood back and watched it, talking quietly. "Look how long it is," said Keesha. "It must be as long as I am!" We watched as the startled snake started to move slowly past us, and then suddenly raced away. We were late for supper that day, but it did not matter because we all had such a great time.

I want to go back to camp next summer and learn as much about nature as Keesha knows. That would be amazing!

1. List the two main elements of the setting.

   Time: _____   Place:_____

2. Match each event from the story to the correct time and place. Draw lines to connect them.

Event	Place	Time
see baby possums	in field	every noon
sing songs	in crook of the beech tree	drizzly day
discover blue racer	in woods	bedtime
sketch plant specimens	in dining hall	second day
hear silly stories	in a national park	one night
observe raccoons	in cabin	fifth day

3. Describe the summer camp by discussing the various activities of the campers.

   _____
   _____
   _____
   _____
   _____

☐ I can use specific details from a text to describe a character, a setting, or an event.
☐ I can read and comprehend grade-level fiction text.

Name_____

Story Elements

What Joy!

Read the story. Answer the questions.

Teddy almost fell out of his seat that Monday afternoon. Mrs. Beeker, his science teacher, announced to the class that they would soon be taking a trip. The following week, they would visit a nearby nature preserve to examine the wildlife in Dilly Pond! That meant Teddy would soon be able to see some leopard frogs!

In his area, leopard frogs could only be found in Dilly Pond. Teddy had watched nature shows about them for years. This would finally be his chance to see them in person.

When the morning of September 25 arrived, the class boarded the bus in front of the school. They rode off to the rural setting of Dilly Pond, which was 18 miles (28.9 km) away. Students snapped pictures of crustaceans and small fish. They sketched pictures of plants along the pond's edge. They observed birds, mammals, and amphibians in the wetlands community. Meanwhile, Teddy tiptoed through reeds, spying on dozens of fabulous frogs. He was in frog heaven!

That was 30 years ago, but Teddy still remembers. As he prepares the science laboratory for his students, his mind returns to that glorious afternoon so many years ago. It was the day that he first knew what he wanted to do with his life. It was one of the best days he could remember.

1. What three scenes are described in the story?

Time	Place
a. _____	_____
b. _____	_____
c. _____	_____

2. What is Teddy's job today? _____

3. How did the class trip affect Teddy? _____

_____

4. Think about Mrs. Beeker. How might she feel about her field trip's influence on Teddy?

_____

_____

- ❑ I can use specific details from a text to describe a character, a setting, or an event.
- ❑ I can compare and contrast the points of view from which different stories are narrated.
- ❑ I can read and comprehend grade-level fiction text.

Listen, My Children

Read the lines of dialogue from different stories. Match each set of quotes with a time and a place.

Time	
on an autumn morning	late one afternoon
in early spring	one summer night
on a wintry day	during baseball season

Place	
in a snowy field	in a big yard
on a beach	on a baseball field
in a living room	in a garden

1. Boom!

   "Look, Dad! Don't those fireworks look pretty over the water? That last one looked like a dandelion."

   Time: _____
   _____
   Place:_____
   _____

2. "OK, do you have your rake?"

   "I sure do. I can't wait to rake those leaves!"

   "Well, I'm glad to have your help as long as you don't jump into the piles when we're done."

   Time: _____
   _____
   Place:_____
   _____

3. "Wow! This is so much fun!"

   "I know. Renting a snowmobile was a great idea."

   "Can you ride toward those trees over there? Then, we'll stop and build a snowman."

   Time: _____
   _____
   Place:_____
   _____

4. "Ooh! See those flowers over there?"

   "What are they called?"

   "Well, the purple ones near that big maple are called lilacs."

   Time: _____
   _____
   Place:_____
   _____

5. "You're out!"

   "What?"

   "You're out of there!"

   "Come on! That wasn't a strike."

   Time: _____
   _____
   Place:_____
   _____

☐ I can use specific details from a text to describe a character, a setting, or an event.

☐ I can read and comprehend grade-level fiction text.

Name_____

Another Place

Read the story. Answer the questions on page 27.

Hello. My name is Ansal Khamba. I am 12 years old and attend a school in the city of Kolkata, India. My parents are both teachers. My father teaches Western literature in a college. If you are American, you might call this a "high school." My mother teaches world studies at the university. Both of my parents have gone to school in other countries as well as India. They have been to Cambridge, England; Cairo, Egypt; Boston, United States; and Bonn, Germany. They say I may go to school overseas if I want. But, I think I will stay in India. We have many good universities here.

My mother says I should tell you something about our country of Bharat. That is the official name of India. It would be difficult to tell you briefly about our country. It is very old and has at least 5,000 years of recorded history. Perhaps I will tell you about some of our beautiful sights instead.

My favorite place is the Taj Mahal. My parents took me there when I was seven years old. The towers of this magnificent structure rise high into the sky. An emperor named Shah Jahan ordered this building be created to honor his dead wife, Mumtaz Mahal. Twenty thousand workers worked 20 years to build this memorial, using white marble and red sandstone. They built reflecting pools and gardens outside.

When I was eight years old, my mother took me on a trip to the Bandhavgarh National Park. She said it was for my educational training. The many birds of the park are beautiful. I loved the blues and greens of the peacocks. The park is most famous for the care and protection it offers to tigers. It has more Bengal tigers than any other place in the world. The park is also home to lots of leopards.

Two years ago, Father and Mother took me to the Thar Desert. What a harsh place! I cannot imagine anyone living in a land like that, yet many people do. They even hold desert festivals there every year. We traveled through the Thar Desert by safari, riding on camels.

This summer, we visited a region called Ladakh. There are many hills and mountains there. My family stayed in the home of a Tibetan family who were gracious hosts. After spending four days getting used to the high altitude, we hiked into the Zaskar Mountains. What a breathtaking view from so high up! We could look down across valleys of fields and villages. There are so many beautiful sights to see in my country!

☐ I can read and comprehend grade-level fiction text.

Another Place (cont.)

Use the story from page 26 to answer the questions.

1. How old was Ansal when he visited each place?

    a. Taj Mahal _____

    b. Thar Desert _____

    c. Bandhavgarh National Park _____

    d. Ladakh _____

2. Write the name of the place that matches each description.

    a. bird sanctuary _____

    b. magnificent structure_____

    c. large tiger population _____

    d. view from a mountain _____

    e. camel ride _____

3. Write a short description of one of the places in this story.

    _____

    _____

    _____

4. What visual would have helped you better understand what was happening in the story?

    _____

    How would it help? _____

5. Read another story about the country of India. Compare the two stories.

    _____

    _____

❏   I can compare and contrast themes, topics, patterns of events in various texts.

❏   I can use the visuals in a text to better understand the subject.

War Heroes

Read the passages about three heroes of World War II. Circle the best summary for each passage. Underline the key ideas that support each summary.

Charles de Gaulle was a French general in the Second World War. When France was invaded by the German army, he escaped to London. While in exile, he formed the French Free Forces. He encouraged the French people to resist the German army. This led to the creation of the French Resistance. Charles de Gaulle continued to lead the French people in their fight for freedom for their nation, until the war ended. He later became the president of France.

1. Which sentence best summarizes the passage above?

   a. Charles de Gaulle was known for his determination.

   b. Charles de Gaulle helped create the French Resistance.

   c. Charles de Gaulle became the president of France.

Virginia Hall was an American living in France during World War II. She had lost her leg several years earlier and wore a wooden prosthetic. Although her wooden leg sometimes made it difficult to get around, she was determined to help stop the Germans. Hall helped train Resistance fighters. She established safe houses. She hid pilots whose planes had been damaged. She also gathered information. To protect her identity, Hall used a code name. Her efforts saved many lives. After the war, she received an award for her heroic service.

2. Which sentence best summarizes the passage above?

   a. Virginia Hall was recognized for her heroic service.

   b. People with physical disabilities can do many things.

   c. Virginia Hall worked for the Resistance during World War II.

Bernard Montgomery was the best-known British general in World War II. He was commander of the British army. He and his troops served in Africa during the war. Nicknamed "Monty," he gave the German army its first defeat in North Africa. Winston Churchill believed the victory turned the tide of the war. Montgomery later led troops in Europe. He continued to fight until the war ended.

3. Which sentence best summarizes the passage above?

   a. Bernard Montgomery was a British general who fought in Africa.

   b. General Montgomery was nicknamed "Monty."

   c. Bernard Montgomery was friends with Winston Churchill.

☐ **I can tell the main idea of a text and use key details to support it.**
☐ **I can read and comprehend grade-level informational text.**

Fireflies

Read the passage. Choose words from the word bank to complete the summary.

Word Bank

adults	chemicals	hatch
insects	light	mates

Fireflies are bioluminescent insects. That means they produce their own light. They do this by combining chemicals in their bodies. When the chemicals mix with oxygen, fireflies light up the rear parts of their bodies.

The purpose of this light is to help the firefly find a mate. Each species of firefly has a special code. The code is made up of a pattern of light. It includes the number and length of flashes and the time between flashes. It also includes the firefly's flight pattern while flashing.

After mating, the female firefly lays about 100 eggs. When the eggs hatch, larvae emerge. The larvae are bioluminescent. They are sometimes called glowworms. The larvae eat during the spring, summer, and autumn months. They sleep through two winters. Then, they progress into the next stage of their lives. They crawl into the soil, where they metamorphose, or change, into pupae. After about two months, they emerge as adult fireflies.

Firefly light is not hot. It is, however, very bright. In some countries, fireflies are used as lanterns. People also release fireflies at festivals. It is fun to watch their bright lights flash in the night sky.

1. Fireflies are bioluminescent _____ . They mix _____

   to produce _____ . That helps fireflies to find _____ .

   After mating, the females lay about 100 eggs. The eggs _____ and larvae

   emerge. The larvae go through different stages until they become _____ .

2. What insects do you see in your area? _____

   _____

3. How do they compare with fireflies?

   _____

   _____

☐	I can figure out the meaning of word or phrases in informational text.
☐	I can compare and contrast themes, topics, and patterns of events.
☐	I can read and comprehend grade-level informational text.

What Is Going On?

Match each story with a summary. Circle the words and phrases in each story that helped you choose the matching summary.

_____ 1.   When we help others selflessly, we grow emotionally.

_____ 2.   Some fears may seem to be irrational.

_____ 3.   Sights, tastes, or smells may trigger memories of past experiences.

_____ 4.   With hard work and determination, we can overcome obstacles.

a.   I do not like mice. I know they are just little animals that cannot hurt me. However, mice petrify me. I do not recall any incident or dream that would cause this fear. I do not even remember ever seeing a live mouse, except in a pet shop. But, if someone even mentions that one may be nearby, I climb on a chair and yell, "Mouse!"

b.   Mark wanted to go to the park with his friends. But, he had promised to walk his neighbor's dog, Riley. Mrs. Conti had had an accident and would not be able to walk for several weeks. Mark thought it would be easy to help her out and walk her dog. He was mistaken. Whatever direction Mark walked, Riley pulled the opposite way. Sometimes, Riley would just sit and refuse to budge. Maybe he is not stubborn but only sad, Mark thought as he sat next to Riley. "It's okay, Riley. Mrs. Conti will be better soon." Riley's brown eyes stared at Mark as if he understood every word. Mark smiled and scratched Riley behind the ears. It felt nice to help out.

c.   Terry sniffed and caught the scent of corn roasting on the neighbor's grill. The aroma reminded him of his time at camp last summer. Terry treasured his memories of hiking in the woods, canoeing, and swimming in the cool, crystal waters of the lake. He had met some of his closest friends at camp. Terry reached for the telephone. It had been a long time since he talked with any of his friends from camp. But, now seemed like an excellent time!

d.   Kami was excited to become the newest member of the track and field team. But, she was worried about it too. Although she loved to run, hurdling made her nervous. One wrong move, and ouch! She told the coach about her concerns. Coach Girard assured her that she would not learn how to hurdle overnight. But, with hard work and practice, she would soon be hurdling like a champ. Kami took the coach's advice. Before she knew it, she could jump over hurdles with confidence and agility.

☐   I can use key details to determine the theme of a text.
☐   I can summarize a text.
☐   I can read and comprehend grade-level fiction text.

Making Matches

Match each set of bulleted sentences to a summary statement in the box.

_____ 1.
- The children groaned when we woke them so early.
- My wife brought a blanket to sit on the ground.
- The sun appeared over the valley.
- It was a magnificent sight to see.

_____ 2.
- This activity teaches responsibility and caring for pets.
- Limited space is needed to raise rabbits.
- Raising rabbits is an excellent way to learn about caring for pets.
- Children also form close bonds with these animals.

a. Having a garden can be very time consuming.

b. Raising rabbits is a valuable experience for children.

c. Torch is a very popular band.

d. This year's vacation to the amusement park was lots of fun.

e. The new lasagna recipe was a hit with the whole family.

f. The sunrise my family experienced was spectacular.

_____ 3.
- We arrived at the gates before the park opened.
- The weather stayed cool and sunny all day long.
- We rode every ride without having to wait in long lines.
- The roller coaster was the ride we enjoyed most.

_____ 4.
- Dad spent three hours preparing lasagna for dinner.
- Mom kept opening the saucepan and sampling the sauce.
- All six of us had two helpings of lasagna.
- There were no leftovers to freeze for lunches.

_____ 5.
- Tadas carefully laid out a plan for each section of his garden.
- The garden store where he bought supplies was very crowded.
- It took five days to prepare the plot and plant sunflower seeds.
- Tadas weeds his garden every Saturday morning.

_____ 6.
- People waited in line for tickets all night.
- Fans of the band, Torch, were willing to pay $100 a ticket.
- The performance had the highest attendance in this stadium.
- Tickets for the concert sold out in less than two hours.

☐ I can use key details to determine the theme of a text.
☐ I can summarize a text.

Name_____

I Plant

Read the poem. Answer the questions.

I have planted a memory tree,
neither too great
nor too small.
A tree for life,
to celebrate the beauty around me
and to remind me.

May this tree of life I have set to Earth
grow roots strongly anchored,
grow branches stretching wide,
to remind me often
of a grandparent's arms
and that loving embrace.

1. Write a summary of the poet's message. _____

_____

_____

2. What does the poet remember? _____

_____

_____

3. What is the poet celebrating? _____

_____

_____

4. Which word is a synonym for *secured*? _____

5. Which words show the poet is joyful? _____

_____

☐   I can summarize a text.
☐   I can figure out the meaning of words and phrases in a text using context
    clues.
☐   I can read and comprehend grade-level fiction text.

Puppy Love

Read the poem. Answer the questions.

My owner is the very best,
She pets and plays and all the rest.
I get the best food in my dish,
She is kinder than I'd ever wish.
I'd never put her to the test.

She loves me true, all of the time,
Even with a coat covered in grime.
Of course, there are times that she scolds,
But I am never left out in the cold.
Her love knows no reason or rhyme.

Even as we both grow up
And I am no longer just a pup,
She will still play and talk to me.
I know two friends we will always be,
Because she is the very best, yup!

1. Which detail should be included in a summary of this poem?
   a. The dog often gets covered in grime.
   b. The dog likes to eat yummy food.
   c. The dog thinks her owner is the best.

2. Which detail should not be included in a summary of this poem?
   a. The dog and her owner will both grow up one day.
   b. The dog likes spending time with her owner.
   c. The owner takes good care of her dog.

3. Name four things the dog loves about her life.

   _____

   _____

4. Using details from the poem, write a summary.

   _____

   _____

   ☐ I can summarize a text.
   ☐ I can use specific details from a text to describe a character, a setting, or an event.
   ☐ I can read and comprehend grade-level fiction text.

Name_____

Early American Indians

Read the passage. Write a summary that includes all of the underlined words from the passage. If you do not know the meaning of an underlined word, use clues from the passage to help you.

Long ago, the northern forests in North America were not good for farming. The early American Indians who lived there hunted and fished for food.

To learn how to survive this way, they played games when they were young. Their games taught them all of the things they needed to know to become hunters and fishermen. For example, they needed to be able to pick up clues and signs from their environment. They played tracking games. They also needed to learn how to conceal themselves among trees, plants, and rocks. So, they played hiding games. In one game, young men threw axes. In another, they took turns throwing spears or sticks into a hoop on the ground. These games improved their accuracy. All of these activities helped them learn how to fish and hunt for food.

As the boys grew into fishermen, they used nets, traps, and spears to fish. With these tools, they caught whitefish and jackfish in lakes. In the rivers, they fished for Arctic grayling and trout. Meanwhile, hunters searched for moose, rabbits, and wolverines.

Young American Indians also had to learn how to adjust to the changing seasons. Hunters and fishermen used different techniques in the summers and winters. During the summers, fishermen caught food from the shores or in canoes. In the winters, they fished through holes cut into the ice. Sometimes, a hunter would discover a hibernating bear in the wintertime. That could feed a camp for several days.

When food became scarce, early American Indians lived on dried meat and fish. They also ate pemmican, a mixture of dried berries, dried meat, and animal fat.

_____

_____

_____

_____

_____

_____

❑ I can summarize a text.
❑ I can figure out the meaning of words and phrases in a text using context clues.
❑ I can read and comprehend grade-level informational text.

Name_____

How Do We See?

Read an explanation of how the human eye sees. Answer the questions.

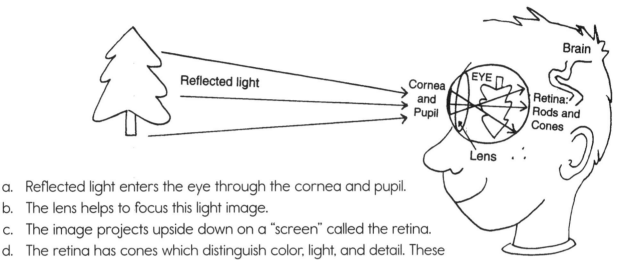

a. Reflected light enters the eye through the cornea and pupil.
b. The lens helps to focus this light image.
c. The image projects upside down on a "screen" called the retina.
d. The retina has cones which distinguish color, light, and detail. These cones are especially useful for daytime vision. They send information to the brain by way of the optic nerve.
e. The retina also has rods which distinguish motion and objects. These rods are very important for nighttime vision. They also send information to the brain via the optic nerve.
f. A person has 20/20 vision if he sees at 20 feet what a person with normal vision can see at 20 feet. A person with 20/200 vision sees at 20 feet what a person with normal vision sees at 200 feet.

1. Summarize how people receive sight. _____

_____

_____

2. What does it mean to have 20/80 vision? _____

_____

_____

3. What does it mean to have 40/20 vision? _____

_____

_____

4. How did the visual help you understand the text? _____

_____

❑ I can use details and examples from a text to explain and draw inferences.
❑ I can use the visuals in a text to better understand the subject.
❑ I can read and comprehend grade-level informational text.

Man in Space

Read this time line showing important dates in the life of Charles Conrad, Jr. Answer the questions.

1930   born in Philadelphia

1953   graduated from Princeton University

1953   entered Navy, completed Navy test for pilot school

1962   became an astronaut

1965   copiloted the *Gemini 5* mission

1966   commanded the *Gemini 11* mission

1969   commanded the *Apollo 12* flight,
        landed module on the moon

1973   served as commander of the first mission of *Skylab*

1974   retired from both Navy and astronaut program

1.   Write a simple summary of the life of Charles Conrad.

_____

_____

_____

2.   When did Conrad first become an astronaut? _____

3.   In what year did he land on the moon? _____

4.   For how many years did he serve in the Navy? _____

5.   Which program came first: *Apollo*, *Gemini*, or *Skylab*?_____

6.   How is this text organized? _____

7.   Do you think Conrad was successful at his career? _____

      Why or why not? _____

      _____

☐   **I can use details and examples from a text to explain and draw inferences.**
☐   **I can explain the way a text is organized.**
☐   **I can read and comprehend grade-level informational text.**

Name_____

Pasteur

Read the passage. Answer the questions.

A famous chemist named Louis Pasteur changed the way scientists think about disease. Pasteur was born in 1822 in Dole, France. He was a doctor of science but not a physician. As a result, many people in the medical profession did not take his work seriously. Pasteur wanted others to know that germs exist and that they cause disease. Eventually, he discovered a cure for a silkworm disease. He also developed vaccines for rabies and anthrax.

Pasteur also changed the way we drink milk. He developed a process called pasteurization as a way to remove germs from wine and beer. This process, called pasteurization after Pasteur, was later used to make milk safe to drink. During pasteurization, liquid is heated to kill any bacteria it contains. But, heat cannot be too high because it could change the taste of the milk.

To pasteurize milk, it must be heated to 140°F (60°C) for 30 minutes. The milk is then cooled quickly and sealed in sterile containers. That gets rid of the germs and preserves the taste.

In his later years, the importance of Pasteur's work was recognized by the medical community. He was often invited to speak at international medical meetings.

Each time you drink a glass of cold, refreshing, germ-free milk, you have Louis Pasteur to thank. And, do not cry if you spill it! Milk is pasteurized each day. So, there is plenty more where that came from.

1. Write a statement that describes Pasteur. _____

   _____

2. What is Pasteur best known for? _____

3. Write a short summary of the passage.

   _____

   _____

   _____

4. What evidence does the author use to support his opinion that Pasteur's work was important?

   _____

   _____

☐ I can summarize the text.
☐ I can explain how the author uses evidence to support the ideas in a text.
☐ I can read grade-level informational text.

Name_____

A Picture-Perfect Moment

Read the cartoon. Answer the questions.

1. Which of the following best summarizes the cartoon?

    a. A father lovingly pushes his daughter on a swing.

    b. A father hurts his head while swinging his daughter.

    c. A daughter learns to swing for the first time.

2. Which detail should be included in a summary of this cartoon?

    a. A mother takes out a camera to take pictures.

    b. A father performs a trick while swinging his daughter.

    c. A daughter does not like being pushed on a swing.

3. What does the word *underdog* mean in this cartoon?

    _____

4. Write a new title for this cartoon.

    _____

☐   I can I can summarize the text.
☐   I can make connections between text and a visual.

38

Wide World of Animals

Read the passage. Underline key details as you read each paragraph. Use those words to write a two-sentence summary for each animal.

Uncle Bob loves animals. He has created a computer library of the animals that he likes best. Here is information about two of his favorites.

Dolphins

These ocean-dwelling mammals live around the world. Dolphins have excellent hearing. They can hear noises at higher frequencies than humans can hear. Dolphins eat fish. They find food using their built in sonar, or echolocation. To do this, they make clicking noises underwater. These noises create sound waves that bounce off objects and echo back, which helps dolphins track and locate prey. A group of dolphins is known as a pod. Scientists consider these creatures to be among the most intelligent of all animals.

_____

_____

_____

Baboons

These primates live in parts of Africa and Arabia. They prefer life on the ground to the tree-climbing life of many of their monkey cousins. Their appearance makes them easy to identify. Baboons have long faces, overhanging brows, and colorful, hairless backsides. They eat small mammals, crustaceans, insects, and other tiny crawling creatures. They also feed on plants and fruit. One kind of baboon grazes on grass. Baboons have large cheek pouches that they use to store food. A group of baboons is called a troop. The size of a troop can range in number from 30 to 100.

_____

_____

_____

Which animal did you find the most interesting? _____

Based on your reading, what questions would you ask Uncle Bob about that animal?

_____

_____

☐ I can tell the main idea of a text and use key details to support it.
☐ I can use information from two sources to write or talk about a subject.
☐ I can read and comprehend grade-level informational text.

Does It Fit?

Read the summaries. Match the correct summary to each supporting sentence by writing the correct letter on the lines.

Summary A: A young wolf roams the woods on her own for the first time.
Summary B: A girl plans a surprise family picnic.
Summary C: The city of Minneapolis has a bustling night life.
Summary D: A boy prepares for his first summer job.

_____ 1. When night falls, the streets fill with people who are eager to enjoy what the city has to offer.

_____ 2. At dawn, the young wolf decided to step out on her own.

_____ 3. He grabbed his uniform out of the dryer and hung it carefully on the hanger.

_____ 4. She pulled the cooler out of the garage and wiped it clean.

_____ 5. It was scary to be out in the woods all alone, but it was exciting too!

_____ 6. He showered and then shaved the few stray hairs growing on his young face.

_____ 7. At concerts, people listen to the music they enjoy.

_____ 8. She found apples and grapes in the refrigerator and rinsed them off.

_____ 9. At theaters, crowds line up to buy tickets to the newest plays.

_____ 10. She rummaged through the linen closet and found a picnic blanket.

_____ 11. She could hear the wind whistle through the trees and the birds singing from the branches as she walked past on her four paws.

_____ 12. He put on the clean uniform and combed his hair.

_____ 13. She packed sandwiches, fruit, cheeses, and pies. Then, she called her family together to share her surprise.

_____ 14. As he walked to the burger stand, he imagined receiving his first paycheck.

☐ I can summarize a text.
☐ I can read and comprehend grade-level fiction text.

Into the West

Read the passage. Write an outline to summarize the passage.

The Shoshoni are an American Indian people. They live in the western part of the United States. Currently, their population numbers about 10,000 people. Long ago, this group traveled the western mountains and valleys. They moved with the seasons to find food. Today, many of them live on reservations.

The Shoshoni believed in a creator god. According to legend, he heard the morning prayer of the people. It lifted to heaven on the rays of the sun. The animals helped the god with his creations. The Shoshoni believed that Coyote made humans.

Hundreds of years ago, there was a Shoshoni woman named Sacagawea. She traveled with Lewis and Clark. She helped them speak with other American Indians. She also helped them find food. She taught them about the western environment too. When their boat capsized, she saved Clark's journals.

The presence of the young woman and her infant son helped ensure peaceful travel. Other American Indians trusted them. After all, if Lewis and Clark were planning to fight, they would not bring a woman and child with them.

Today, Sacagawea's face appears on a dollar coin. She and the Shoshoni people are an important part of American history.

1. **The Shoshoni People of America**

I. _____

II. _____

III. _____

IV. _____

V. _____

VI. _____

2. How does an outline help to show the important parts of a summary?

_____

_____

☐ I can summarize the text.
☐ I can explain the way a text is organized.
☐ I can read and comprehend grade-level informational text.

Name_____

Mystery of the Disappearing Lunches

Read the passage. Answer the questions.

As soon as we were old enough, we each became responsible for packing our own lunches. My five brothers made all of their lunches and I did too. But, having five brothers in the kitchen every morning equals chaos! I started making my lunch the night before when things were calm and quiet.

One Sunday night, I made my favorite lunch and stored the bag in the refrigerator. When I went to grab it on Monday morning, it was gone! Mom asked all of my brothers, and each one denied taking my lunch.

I would have let it go, but the next morning, my lunch was missing again. Every day for a week, I had to make lunch in a rush because the one I had prepared the night before was gone.

My brothers can be annoying sometimes, but they are always honest. Mom wanted to believe them, but she also wanted to find out what was happening. She decided to talk to Dad about it. She had been trying not to bother him with too many problems because he had been working a lot of overtime hours lately. But, this was becoming increasingly frustrating. Should she ground all of the boys? Should she just give me lunch money?

Mom told Dad about the situation that night at the dinner table while we all sat eating. I was astonished to see Dad blush a little! Dad cleared his throat and then said, "Oh, those lunches weren't meant for me? I thought you were saving me time by packing mine since I've been leaving at five in the morning." Who could have guessed that Dad was the culprit? Our mouths dropped open in shock for a moment. Then, we all burst out laughing!

The mystery of my missing lunches was solved. Mom offered to make Dad his lunch on the days he worked overtime, and my brothers were off the hook.

1. Use the details in the story to write a brief summary. Put events in sequential order.

    _____

    _____

    _____

2. How was Dad's point of view different from the narrator's view? _____

    _____

3. Is the narrator a boy or a girl? _____

    How do you know? _____

    _____

☐ I can use details and examples in a text to explain and draw inferences.
☐ I can summarize the text.
☐ I can compare and contrast the points of view from which different stories are narrated.

A Dirty Deal

Read the letter. Answer the questions.

42 Current Ave.
Howell, MI 48843
February 12, 2015

Dear Sir or Madam,

Last fall, I purchased your much publicized video game *Jungle Adventure*. In your television commercials, you claim that this game would put you "in the middle of a jungle."

First, the package arrived late. I ordered it online on October 5, but it did not arrive until December 4, well past the five-day delivery guarantee. Second, the game did not produce the sounds of slurping mud or sliding quicksand that was described in your commercials. Third, every time the hero makes it safely to the Monkey's Mambo on level four, the game freezes.

Finally, last Tuesday, the game caused a meltdown of my entire gaming system. I was entering a cave I discovered, not far from the Mud Monkey's Lair, when the screen became wavy. A text frame appeared reading, "Got You, Dude!" Fifteen seconds later, smoke poured out of my gaming system, and it was completely broken.

Since I lost everything, I request two things of you. The first is a reimbursement for the game. The second is a down payment toward the purchase of a new gaming system.

With Dismay,
Jack Dram

1. Which of these statements best summarizes the intent of the letter?

   a. A buyer wishes to congratulate a company for keeping promises about its product.

   b. A buyer wishes to return a game that failed to meet expectations.

   c. A buyer wishes to receive his money back for a video game that was faulty.

2. What are the four complaints of the letter writer?

   a. _____

   b. _____

   c. _____

   d. _____

   ☐ I can use details to determine the theme of a text.
   ☐ I can summarize the text.
   ☐ I can read and comprehend grade-level fiction text.

Name_____

Same or Different?

Compare and contrast the two pictures. List the differences between them.

A.

B.

Example: There are two craters behind
        the house.

1. _____
2. _____
3. _____
4. _____
5. _____
6. _____
7. _____
8. _____
9. _____
10. _____

Example: There are three craters behind
        the house.

1. _____
2. _____
3. _____
4. _____
5. _____
6. _____
7. _____
8. _____
9. _____
10. _____

☐   I can compare and contrast themes, topics, and patterns of events in various
       texts.

44

Name_____

This and That

Analogies compare things. Read each phrase and fill in the blank with a word that completes each analogy.

1. **Chirp** is to **bird** as _____ is to **dog**.

2. **Spoon** is to **bowl** as **straw** is to _____.

3. **Hair** is to **human** as _____ is to **rabbit**.

4. **Pencil** is to **write** as **paintbrush** is to _____.

5. **Dry** is to **desert** as _____ is to **ocean**.

6. **Rink** is to **hockey** as _____ is to **football**.

7. **Water** is to **pool** as _____ is to **balloon**.

8. **A** is to **B** as **C** is to _____.

Draw a picture to complete each analogy. Fill in the missing word.

9. Engineer   is to   train   as   pilot   is to _____.

   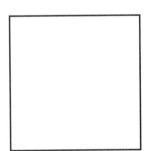

10. Hive   is to _____ as   nest   is to _____.

☐   I can compare and contrast themes, topics, and patterns of events in various texts.

Name_____

How Is . . . ?

Circle the letter of each correct answer.

1. How is a desktop computer like a castle?
    a. Both have drawbridges.
    b. Both have towers.
    c. Both have staircases.

2. How is using the Internet like flying?
    a. You use an airplane.
    b. You need a pressurized cabin.
    c. You can reach faraway people and places very quickly.

3. How is a CD like a rainbow?
    a. It can show the colors of the spectrum.
    b. It is shaped the same.
    c. It forms in the rain.

4. How is a computer mouse like a real mouse?
    a. It moves around swiftly and quietly.
    b. It needs cheese.
    c. It has teeth.

5. How is the computer age like the time of the Sumerians, who used clay tablets to communicate?
    a. Sumerians invented computers.
    b. A new way to record information was invented.
    c. We write on clay tablets.

6. How is Web research like hunting for objects?
    a. You need to decide on a goal.
    b. You need to gather clues on the way.
    c. both A and B

7. How is surfing the Internet like looking at the world from space?
    a. The print is small.
    b. It can give you a different perspective.
    c. You need a spaceship.

☐   I can compare and contrast themes, topics, and patterns of events in various texts.

Where Do I Find It?

Read the examples of reference books and their purposes. For questions 2–5, write the letter of the resource book the person should use. For questions 6–7, write the names of the resources.

a. almanac: facts and information about a specific year
b. atlas: maps of regions, countries, states, and provinces
c. encyclopedia: detailed information about many topics
d. thesaurus: words and their synonyms and antonyms
e. dictionary: words and their meanings

Example:

What is a zither?

1. She should use a/an _e_.

Where is Tierra del Fuego?

2. He should use a/an _____.

I want to know more about ladybugs.

3. She should use a/an _____.

What was the #1 song on the day I was born?

4. She should use a/an _____.

What is the opposite of the word "serendipitous"?

5. He should use a/an _____.

6.   What references would be most useful for writing a report and making a poster about China?

_____

7.   What references would be useful for writing a poem using adjectives that mean *great*?

_____

☐   I can figure out the meaning of words or phrases in informational text.
☐   I can use information from two sources to write or talk about a subject.

Something Is Not Right

Read each group of words. For questions 1–7, fill in the circle of the item that does not belong. For questions 8–13, circle the letter of the answer that tells what the items have in common.

1. ◯ horse   ◯ beagle   ◯ collie   ◯ terrier
2. ◯ car   ◯ truck   ◯ convertible   ◯ pyramid
3. ◯ George Washington   ◯ Abraham Lincoln   ◯ Theodore Roosevelt   ◯ Danny
4. ◯ happy   ◯ disappointed   ◯ glad   ◯ delighted
5. ◯ delighted   ◯ miserable   ◯ neighbor   ◯ anxious
6. ◯ walked   ◯ hurried   ◯ crawled   ◯ married
7. ◯ tail   ◯ paw   ◯ muzzle   ◯ jeans

8. joyful, miserable, anxious

    a. happiness   b. sadness   c. emotions

9. war, argument, disagreement

    a. conflict   b. harmony   c. nation

10. hamsters, cats, dogs

    a. amphibians   b. reptiles   c. pets

11. car, truck, sedan

    a. dogs   b. vehicles   c. sandwiches

12. tail, paw, fur

    a. parts of a dog   b. parts of a person   c. parts of a car

13. muzzle, snout, beak

    a. noses   b. ears   c. eyes

☐ I can figure out the meaning of words or phrases in informational text.
☐ I can read and comprehend grade-level informational text.

DVDs for Everyone

Read the movie descriptions. Choose a movie title for each customer. Write it on the line.

Animated *Adventures of Mama Llama*—for ages 2–10: Mamma Llama travels from her mountain home to the city, meeting many silly animals along the way.
Comedy *The Magic Baseball*—for ages 7 and up: A young boy finds a baseball that never misses the bat, and he makes it to the World Series.
Musical *Dance until You Drop*—for ages 10 and up: A group of clumsy teenagers try to enter a dancing competition.
Drama *Olden Days*—for ages 18 and up: Two army veterans reflect on their childhoods in a sentimental and heartwarming story.
Drama *Holiday Happenings*—for ages 7 and up: Family members make a holiday happy and special.
Romance *Together Forever*—for ages 18 and up: Two people with different backgrounds fall in love despite obstacles from their families.

"My brother and I are sports fans!"

1.   I recommend: _____

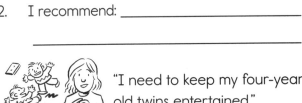

"I like upbeat movies with lots of music!"

2.   I recommend: _____
_____

"My husband and I want a film with some history."

3.   I recommend: _____
_____

"I need to keep my four-year-old twins entertained."

4.   I recommend: _____
_____

"It is our anniversary, and we want something romantic."

5.   I recommend: _____
_____

☐   **I can use specific details from a text to describe a character, a setting, or an event.**
☐   **I can read and comprehend grade-level fiction text.**

Analogies

Circle the letter in front of each correct answer.

1. **Telescope** is to **star** as **microscope** is to _____ .

   a. planet   b. glass   c. cell

2. **In** is to **import** as **out** is to _____ .

   a. exit   b. exult   c. export

3. **Assertive** is to **passive** as **definite** is to _____ .

   a. vague   b. exact   c. define

4. **Evil** is to **malevolent** as **good** is to _____ .

   a. sullen   b. benevolent   c. relentless

5. **Hate** is to **detest** as **love** is to _____ .

   a. fear   b. adore   c. tolerate

6. **Reveal** is to **divulge** as **hide** is to _____ .

   a. discover   b. imagine   c. conceal

7. **Observe** is to **observation** as **condense** is to _____ .

   a. condenser   b. condensation   c. watch

8. **Gratitude** is to **ingratitude** as **grateful** is to _____ .

   a. ungrateful   b. thankful   c. gratefully

☐ I can figure out the meaning of words and phrases in informational text.
☐ I can use information from two sources to write or talk about a subject.

Snow Day

Read the following poems. Read each numbered statement. Write **a** if the statement applies to the first poem. Write **b** if the statement applies to the second poem. Write **c** if it applies to both poems. Write **d** if it applies to neither poem.

a. The children awoke to a happy sight,
    While they were sleeping, the world had turned white.
    Their mother peered into their room and said,
    "No school today. Go back to bed!"

b. Father heard the news from his bed
    And pulled the pillow over his head.
    Slipping on the ice,
    Is not very nice!
    He wished it was summer instead.

1. The weather is seen as annoying. _____

2. A different season is desired. _____

3. Winter is welcomed. _____

4. The setting is winter. _____

5. The poem takes place at midnight. _____

6. The main idea of the poem is how snow forms. _____

7. The main idea of the poem is a reaction to snow. _____

8. The subject of the poem will have to get up soon. _____

9. The subject of the poem can go back to sleep. _____

10. The poem mentions an item from a bedroom. _____

11. On another piece of paper, write a dialogue that the father and son might have about winter.

- [ ] I can explain the differences between poems, drama, or prose.
- [ ] I can compare and contrast two points of view from which different stories are narrated.
- [ ] I can read and comprehend grade-level fiction text.

Name_____

Mystery of the Missing Jam

Read the story. Answer the questions on page 53.

"I left the jam right here on the table," said Kay, exasperated. "Now, it is gone!"

"The bread is gone too," said Daniel. "Hey, someone left the silverware drawer open. You know how Mom does not like that." He shut the drawer.

"The back door is not closed all the way." Kay opened the door wider. She and Daniel walked out into the backyard and looked around cautiously.

"Do you think someone came into the house?" Daniel asked, looking worried.

Kay smiled. "Someone coming into the house just to take bread, jam, and a few pieces of silverware? I do not think that is very likely." She glanced around again.

Daniel noticed a glinting object on the deck steps. "Look over there! It is one of our knives."

Kay walked down to pick it up. She looked at it closely. "Still clean," she said.

Daniel stared past his sister at the newly dug flower bed. "Somebody has been walking through all that mud." He bent down to look. "Someone with very small feet," he added.

"Now we are getting somewhere," said Kay. "I think we both know who is behind this!" She

followed the footprints, which came to an abrupt end at the edge of the flower bed.

Scanning the rest of the yard, Daniel pointed at the potting shed. There was a muddy footprint on its stone step.

Quietly, Daniel and Kay crept toward the shed. Slowly, they opened the door, knowing they would see the person inside.

When they looked inside the shed, they found Nikki sitting on the floor, her face covered with jam.

Since she had lost the knife on the trip from the kitchen, she was spreading jam on pieces of bread with her fingers.

Kay sighed. "Looks like bath time for you, kid! You're a mess."

Nikki just smiled happily and said, "Jam!"

☐   I can read and comprehend grade-level fiction text.

© Carson-Dellosa • CD-104661

Mystery of the Missing Jam (cont.)

Use the story on page 52 to answer the questions.

1. Which sibling is more observant? Circle your answer.   Kay   Daniel

   List three reasons for your choice:

   a. _____

   b. _____

   c. _____

2. Fill in the chart. Write a conclusion for each clue. Compare the clues. Star the clue you felt was most helpful to Kay and Daniel in solving the "mystery." Circle the clue that was most important in showing the location of Nikki.

Mystery Clues and Conclusions	
Clue	Conclusion
a. finding the knife on the deck steps	a. The person had gone down the steps.
b. a clean knife was found	b.
c. small footprints in the flower bed	c.
d. a muddy footprint on the shed step	d.

3. a. Who is the youngest? Circle your answer.   Kay   Daniel   Nancy

   b. How do you know? _____

   _____

4. a. Who do you think is the oldest? Circle your answer.   Kay   Daniel   Nancy

   b. Why do you think so? _____

   _____

☐ I can use specific details from a text to describe a character, a setting, or an event.

☐ I can read and comprehend grade-level fiction text.

Name_____

Family Differences

Look at the picture. Write the name of the correct brother or sister in each blank.

Jake   Julia   Joey Jimmy   Jessica   Jordan   Josh

1. _____ is the youngest in the family.

2. _____ has the longest hair.

3. _____ has her hair in two pigtails and Jessica's is in one braided ponytail.

4. _____ looks the most athletic.

5. _____ is the boy who appears to read more than Josh.

6. _____ is the boy taller than Jordan.

7. _____ has the least hair.

8. _____ 's skirt is shorter than _____ 's.

9. _____ is the girl taller than the twins.

10. Julia is taller than _____ .

11. _____ and _____ are of similar height and are not identical twins.

☐   I can use the visuals in a text to better understand the subject.

Name_____

Letter Writing

Read the chart. Compare the types of letters. Write **P** beneath each personal letter. Write **B** beneath each business letter.

Business Letters	Personal Letters
Application: In this type of letter, you ask for a job.	Social: This letter is to send or accept an invitation.
Inquiry: This letter asks about an order or product.	Congratulatory: You write this to say, "Great job!"
Order: This is a letter making a purchase.	Conversational: This letter sends news to friends.
Acknowledgement: You write this letter to say you have received something that was sent to you.	Thank-you: You write this letter to thank someone for a gift, a meal, or another kind act.

Dear Sir:

I have received the web that I ordered, and I am not happy with it. It does not appear strong enough to lasso any kind of tuffet on the market. Please let me know what I need to do to ship it back to you . . .

_____

Dear Tweedledee,

Things sure are dull here without you. The Mad Hatter did say he's planning a party soon, though. The Red Queen tried to ride my motorcycle the other day . . .

_____

Dear Madam:

A friend advised me that you are looking for a nanny. I have excellent references from the Banks family, and I am able to travel via my own umbrella. However, I first need to know . . .

_____

Read the letter. Write your reply.

Dear Lucky Prizewinner:

 Congratulations! The Captain Hook Travel Agency has chosen YOU as the winner of our **"Travel One Way to Paradise"** trip. Please let us know immediately if you would like to fly away to be our honored guest at a tropical feast, featuring a genuine crocodile and other surprises! **The clock is ticking—answer today!**

Your reply: _____

_____

_____

I can compare themes, topics, and patterns in various texts.

© Carson-Dellosa • CD-104661

55

Matter Matters

Read the paragraph. Answer the questions.

Matter makes up everything around us. Matter takes up space and has weight. There are three states of matter: solid, liquid, and gas. Solids have a definite volume and shape. The shape of a solid is not easy to change. The small particles that make up a solid are firmly linked to each other. Liquids have a definite volume but no definite shape. They take on the shape of the container that holds them. The particles in liquids move more slowly than those of gases, and they stick together in bunches. Gases have no definite volume or shape. Their particles move very quickly and are far apart from each other.

1. Write the states of matter in order from most solid to least solid.

    a. _____ b. _____ c. _____

Circle the word or phrase that best fits in each of the sentences.

2. Gas particles move (faster, slower) than liquid particles.

3. A person can walk through a (gas, solid), because the particles are far apart.

4. A solid has a definite (shape, color), but a liquid does not.

5. When water is at room temperature, it (has a definite shape, does not have a definite shape).

6. When water freezes, its shape (cannot be easily changed, can be easily changed).

7. When water evaporates, it (has a definite shape or volume, does not have a definite shape or volume).

Fill in the chart below. Use examples other than the ones already mentioned above.

State of Matter	Definite Shape?	Definite Volume?	Example
Solid	8.	yes	9.
Liquid	10.	11.	12.
Gas	no	13.	14.

15. What kind of resource could you use to find out more information about matter?

_____

16. What search terms would help you find appropriate resources? _____

_____

❑ I can use specific information in nonfiction text to explain the main idea.
❑ I can use information from two sources to write or talk about a subject.
❑ I can read and comprehend grade-level informational text.

Analogies

Complete each analogy. Draw pictures to represent the analogies in questions 14 and 15.

1. **Hudson** is to **river** as **Erie** is to _____ .

2. **One** is to **unicycle** as **two** is to _____ .

3. **Meow** is to **cat** as _____ is to **pig**.

4. **Racket** is to **tennis** as _____ is to **baseball**.

5. **Syrup** is to **pancake** as **frosting** is to _____ .

6. **Baby** is to **adult** as _____ is to **dog**.

7. **Jet** is to **pilot** as _____ is to **conductor**.

8. **English** is to the **United Kingdom** as _____ is to **China**.

9. **Squeak** is to **mouse** as **roar** is to _____ .

10. **Hat** is to **head** as _____ is to **foot**.

11. **Tie** is to **laces** as **zip** is to _____ .

12. **Stop** is to **go** as **begin** is to _____ .

13. **Black** is to **white** as _____ is to **day**.

14. House is to person as shell is to turtle.

	is to		as		is to	

15. Wheel is to wagon as tire is to car.

	is to		as		is to	

❑ I can compare and contrast themes, topics, and patterns.

Fact or Opinion?

Read each sentence. Decide if it is fact or opinion. Circle your answer.

1. Friends are the most important thing in the world.

   fact   opinion

2. Kittens are cute.

   fact   opinion

3. Santa Barbara is in California.

   fact   opinion

4. Air hockey is fun.

   fact   opinion

5. Tadpoles need water to survive.

   fact   opinion

6. Tadpoles turn into frogs.

   fact   opinion

7. It is always a good idea to save wild animals.

   fact   opinion

8. When there is not enough rain there is often a drought.

   fact   opinion

9. A eucalyptus is a tree.

   fact   opinion

10. Choose a fact from the statements above. Write an opinion about that fact.

    _____

11. Choose an opinion from the statements above. Write a fact about the topic.

    _____

☐ **I can read and comprehend grade-level informational text.**

Name_____

A House Divided

Read the passage. Answer the questions.

The year was 1860. The United States was about to go to war with itself. What were the problems? One major issue was slavery. Slavery existed mainly in the South. Slaves worked on large farms. In the North there were not as many farms. Slavery was not permitted in the North. People who tried to outlaw slavery were called **abolitionists**. One group from the North wanted slavery to be illegal in the United States.

Another problem between the North and the South was the way people made money. The North wanted high **tariffs**. Tariffs are taxes charged by the federal government for goods imported into the country. The North had more people and was wealthier than the South. The money from tariffs contributed greatly to projects like new railroads for the North. New railroads were making the North rich.

The Southern states were more rural. They were dependent on farm crops and not industries. The South wanted low tariffs in order to keep selling cotton to other countries like England. The South felt that low tariffs would continue to encourage trade between the United States and other countries. High tariffs would put a burden on countries who wanted to trade with the United States.

The South wanted stronger states' rights. Then, each state could make its own laws. Lincoln was the new president. His Republican party was on the side of the North.

Write **S** after each phrase or statement that describes the South. Write **N** after each phrase or statement that describes the North.

1. wanted high tariffs _____
2. slave labor _____
3. new railroads _____
4. abolitionists _____
5. stronger states' rights _____
6. industrial _____
7. mostly farms _____
8. depended on crops _____

9. Contrast how the North and the South felt about stronger states' rights as opposed to being subject to federal laws._____

_____

_____

10. Do you think the author favored the North or the South in this passage? _____

What evidence from the text supports your answer? _____

_____

☐ I can use specific information in nonfiction text to explain the main idea.
☐ I can explain how the author uses evidence to support the ideas in a text.

You Pick

Each picture shows an effect. Circle the correct cause.

1. Why does the dog bark?

   a. He smells food.

   b. He hears the mailman.

   c. He is ready for a walk.

2. Why is Marti so happy?

   a. She's excited about tomorrow's race.

   b. She's going to the movie theater.

   c. She did well on a test.

3. Why is Henry wet?

   a. He fell into a pool.

   b. Maddie dumped water on his head.

   c. He recently took a shower.

4. Why does Tasha scowl?

   a. She let a goal slip through.

   b. Her pet python is ill.

   c. Her friend spilled milk on her.

5. Why can't Mrs. Collins sleep?

   a. Her husband is snoring.

   b. Her baby is crying.

   c. Her pillow is missing.

☐   I can use the visuals in a text to better understand the subject.

The Right Cause

Look at the causes by the pictures. Read the effects in the effect bank. Match three effects to each cause. Write the letter of each effect in the correct balloon.

Effect Bank

a. has never been beaten in wrestling.

b. punches holes in titanium with his fist.

c. volunteers to babysit for free.

d. can pick up Neanderthal Nate.

e. helps me with homework.

f. does extra chores to help around the house.

1. Captain Colossal is the strongest human on Earth. He . . .

2. My friend is so kind! She . . .

☐ I can use details and examples in a text to explain and draw inferences.

☐ I can compare and contrast themes, topics, and patterns of events in various texts.

Name_____

Caption Capers

Match each cause to the correct effect.

Causes

Effects

1.

_____

2.

_____

3.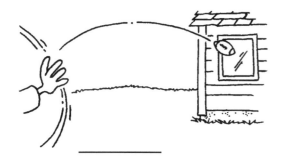

_____

4.

_____

a. Tomás went to Mrs. Kater's front door to apologize.

b. The fruit drink tasted gross.

c. Betsy was tired the next day.

d. Derek ran away.

☐ I can use illustrations and other visuals to support what I know about a text.

Name_____

More Caption Capers

Match each effect to the correct cause.

Effects

Causes

1.

_____

a. Because Bart's wife takes long showers . . .

b. Because Marianne hit a home run . . .

c. Because a storm was coming . . .

d. Because the car ran out of gas . . .

2.

_____

3.

_____

4.

_____

☐ I can use illustrations and other visuals to support what I know about a text.

Cause and Effect

The Lion and the Mouse

Read a version of Aesop's fable. Match each cause to the correct effect.

A lion was sleeping peacefully when he felt something scurry across his giant, velvety paws. He opened his large, amber eyes to see a little mouse standing on its hind legs, staring back at him. The small creature appeared to be frozen with terror.

"How dare you wake me from my slumber?" roared the lion. "Tonight, I shall dine upon fresh mouse so that at least I might have a snack for this inconvenience."

The mouse shivered and cried out, "Please forgive me, King Lion. Spare my life. One day, I may have the opportunity to repay your great kindness by saving your life."

The lion looked at the tiny mouse and felt the corners of his mouth twitch. The very idea of the miniscule rodent saving his life was the most hilarious thing he had ever heard. His mouth opened, and the mouse prepared for the end; but instead of being eaten, the lion let loose a deep, rich laugh. Tears of laughter ran down his regal face. "Go, Sir Mouse. You are too entertaining to eat."

Seasons passed, and one day, while the mouse was scavenging for food, he came upon a horrible sight. The lion was bound head to tail by thick, strong ropes. Exhausted from fighting his bonds, the lion lay motionless—helpless and defeated. The mouse scurried up to the lion's nose and said, "I am here to repay my debt." He chewed and gnawed at the ropes that bound the lion until the great beast was free. The lion stood, stretched, and shook his glorious mane. He lowered his noble head in respect to the mouse and said, "Your debt has been paid, and I thank you."

Causes	Effects
_____ 1. The mouse walked on the lion's paws.	a. The lion was free.
_____ 2. The mouse pleaded for his life.	b. The lion awoke.
_____ 3. The mouse chewed through the ropes.	c. The lion could not escape.
_____ 4. Hunters tied the lion with rope.	d. The lion let the mouse live.

❑ I can use specific details from a text to describe a character, a setting, or an event.

❑ I can read and comprehend grade-level fiction text.

Up and Away!

Read the effect in each box. A list of causes is below. Match three causes to each effect. Write the letter of each cause in the correct box.

Calvin stayed in his house	We traded in our old car
because _____	because _____
because _____	because _____
because _____	because _____
The snake crawled into the hole	We played soccer
because _____	because _____
because _____	because _____
because _____	because _____

a. we needed exercise.

b. it was disliked by Mom.

c. it was scared by a hawk.

d. we needed a van to haul kids.

e. it needed engine repair.

f. it is a game we love.

g. he was catching a cold.

h. it needed sleep after a big meal.

i. he wanted to watch his favorite TV show.

j. it was too chilly to play outside.

k. it was a beautiful, sunny day.

l. it was preparing to hibernate.

☐ I can use specific details from a text to describe a character, a setting, or an event.

Now, I Understand

Underline the cause and circle the effect in each sentence.

1. When Omar stubbed his toe, he cried out, "Ouch!"

2. The rain was coming into the house, so we shut the windows.

3. Because I was full from the tasty chicken soup, I slept like a baby.

4. Karen was disappointed when she missed an easy layup.

5. We made a model volcano for a science fair. It erupted when we mixed vinegar and baking soda.

6. At the airport, David could not sit still because he was excited to fly for the first time.

7. When the theater lights were turned on, I was blinded for a moment.

8. Because he is interested in modern art, Ted begged to see the newest art exhibit.

9. Tanya said, "Go fish!" because she had no kings.

☐   I can use specific details from a text to describe a character, a setting, or an event.

☐   I can read and comprehend grade-level fiction text.

Boy Meets Reality

Read the six effects. Match each effect to the correct set of causes. Write the effect on each line.

Effects

He took too long in the bathroom.   He went shopping.

He was late to school.   He went to the beach.

He saw a movie.   He got an A+ on the assignment.

1. The humidity was unbearable.
    The summer sun shone fiercely.
    Abel was free to relax.
    Effect: _____

2. Cody had no good clothes.
    He needed school supplies.
    He hoped to see friends at the mall.
    Effect: _____

3. Everyone else had seen it.
    Dani offered to take him.
    Emmett just received his allowance.
    Effect: _____

4. Pablo could not find his books.
    He overslept again.
    He took a long time eating breakfast.
    Effect: _____

5. Owen showered for 40 minutes.
    He played with his hair for 10 minutes.
    He stood before the mirror for 20 minutes.
    Effect: _____

6. Lamar went to the media lab.
    He organized his notes.
    He followed the instructions.
    Effect: _____

☐   I can use specific details from a text to describe a character, a setting, or an event.

☐   I can read and comprehend grade-level fiction text.

Traveling with the Corps

Underline the cause and circle the effect in each sentence. Then, answer the question.

1. Because President Jefferson was interested in finding a water route for trade to the Pacific Ocean, he commissioned an expedition called the Corps of Discovery.

2. Sacagawea joined the Corps of Discovery when her husband Toussaint Charbonneau was hired as a guide.

3. Because she was Shoshone, Sacagawea could help Lewis and Clark's expeditionary force obtain food and supplies from her people.

4. As they began, Sacagawea carried her son on her back because he was only a baby.

5. To move the expedition's freight upriver, the group hired a large keelboat.

6. Because of her herbal knowledge, Sacagawea's tasks included gathering edible plants for the Corps.

7. The young woman was surprised when she met her older brother, now a chief among her people.

8. Because her husband was officially hired by the expedition and she was not, Sacagawea received no personal compensation for her work.

9. There are conflicting reports about Sacagawea's later life, so historians consider her a puzzle.

10. What is the best description of how the story about Sacagawea is structured?

    a. Compare and contrast

    b. Sequence of events

    c. Problem and solution

- ☐   I can explain the way a text is organized.
- ☐   I can read and comprehend grade-level informational text.

Instantly Hot and Cold

Read the passage. Answer the questions.

Have you ever been injured and used an instant hot or cold pack? Instant hot and cold packs use a chemical reaction to help you with your sprained ankle or sore back.

A chemical reaction occurs when two chemical substances mix and form different substances. Sometimes, a chemical reaction releases heat. When a chemical called calcium chloride is mixed with water, the reaction releases heat and makes the container feel warm.

Sometimes, a chemical reaction absorbs heat from the environment. When a chemical called ammonium nitrate is mixed with water, the reaction absorbs heat. The container feels cold.

Instant hot and cold packs are plastic pouches filled with a dry chemical—usually calcium chloride or ammonium nitrate. Inside the pouch is another pouch filled with water. When the hot or cold pack is squeezed, the inner pouch breaks. Shaking the instant pack helps the water mix completely with the chemical. A chemical reaction occurs, and the instant pack becomes either hot or cold.

1. You might need a hot or cold pack because _____

    _____ .

2. You might use a pack with calcium chloride because _____

    _____ .

3. You might use a pack with ammonium nitrate because _____

    _____ .

4. You must squeeze the hot or cold pack to _____

    _____ .

5. You must shake a hot or cold pack to _____

    _____ .

6. In one sentence, tell the main idea of the text.

    _____

    _____

☐ **I can use specific information in nonfiction text to explain the main idea.**
☐ **I can read and comprehend grade-level informational text.**

What Caused It?

Read each effect. Write two possible causes for each effect.

1. Trisha's lunch box was empty.

   _____

   _____

2. Sadaf had no homework to do this weekend.

   _____

   _____

3. Caleb felt nauseous.

   _____

   _____

4. The chocolate-colored dog was wet.

   _____

   _____

5. The cornbread burned.

   _____

   _____

6. The coyote howled.

   _____

   _____

7. On another sheet of paper, write a story based on one of the above effects and its cause.

❑ **I can use details and examples in a text to explain and draw inferences.**

What Happened?

Look at each set of causes. Write the effect you might expect.

1. The child stretched the balloon.

   He put it to his lips.

   He pursed his lips around the balloon's neck.

   Effect: _____

2. She was in such a hurry riding her bike.

   She carried her viola across the handlebars.

   She failed to see the rock on the street in front of her.

   Effect: _____

3. We had a tremendous snowstorm during the night.

   Winds gusted to 45 mph (72 kmh).

   The roads are blocked.

   Effect: _____

4. I ran as fast as I could.

   I passed all the other runners.

   I was not even tired.

   Effect: _____

5. I awoke late and was still half asleep.

   I pulled out my toothbrush.

   I smeared hair gel over the bristles.

   Effect: _____

6. Dani held her burger in her hand, even though she had already eaten a large lunch.

   Her pup looked up at her with those begging eyes.

   Sighing, the dog rested his head on her lap.

   Effect: _____

- [ ] **I can use details and examples in a text to explain and draw inferences.**
- [ ] **I can read and comprehend grade-level fiction text.**

Sweeter Than Honey

Scientists make **conclusions** from their observations. The conclusion is the effect. The observations are the causes. Read the numbered set of observations. Match a conclusion to each set.

Conclusions

Bee colonies are complex.

Farmers depend on bees.

Flowering plants are vital to bees.

Bees are diverse insects.

1. Pollen is a protein source.

    Pollen is also a food source for bee larvae.

    Flower nectar is an energy source.

    Conclusion: _____

2. Bees are found in most world regions.

    Bees may be yellow, black, gray, blue, red, or green.

    Bees may range from .08 inches to 1.57 inches (2 mm to 4 cm) in length.

    Conclusion: _____

3. Semisocial bees live in colonies of two to seven.

    Each group consists of a queen and her daughter workers.

    Such colonies are temporary and can change.

    Conclusion: _____

4. Some bees produce honey.

    Beeswax is harvested from honeycombs to sell.

    Bees provide pollination required for many fruits and vegetables.

    Conclusion: _____

5. What is the main idea of this text? _____

☐   I can use specific information in nonfiction text to explain the main idea.
☐   I can read and comprehend grade-level informational text.

© Carson-Dellosa • CD-104661

Picking the Cause

Read each pair of sentences. Circle the cause.

1.   Madison and Ryan were late.

     The bus had a flat tire.

2.   Josh needed help.

     He emailed Dylan.

3.   Josh could not find his watch.

     It had slipped under his dresser.

4.   Josh looked everywhere in his room.

     He hoped to find his grandfather's watch.

5.   Dylan led the way to the house.

     He had the address.

6.   The members of the Mystery Society were excited.

     It was their first case in a long time.

7.   Ryan and Madison ran.

     They were late.

8.   The house had a messy yard.

     It needed a lot of work.

9.   The dresser was in Josh's room.

     Josh took the Mystery Society upstairs.

10. Dylan looked under the dresser.

     The Mystery Society had cracked another case!

11. On another sheet of paper, write a brief summary explaining the main idea behind the story.

☐ I can use details to determine the theme of a text.
☐ I can summarize the text.

What Happened and Why?

Read each sentence. Write the cause and effect. Write an inference about each person.

1. a. Andre earned money by mowing lawns for his neighbors.

    Cause: _____

    Effect:_____

    b. Andre saved his earnings until he could afford to buy a new bike.

    Cause: _____

    Effect:_____

    c. Inference: _____

2. a. Becca forgot to water the plant on her windowsill, and the plant wilted.

    Cause: _____

    Effect:_____

    b. The plant became healthy when Becca watered it.

    Cause: _____

    Effect:_____

    c. Inference: _____

3. a. Having studied very hard, Carla finished the test easily.

    Cause: _____

    Effect:_____

    b. Carla made a perfect score on the test, which brought her grade to an A.

    Cause: _____

    Effect:_____

    c. Inference: _____

❑ I can use details and examples in a text to explain and draw inferences.
❑ I can read and comprehend grade-level fiction text.

Emilio

Read each pair of sentences. Write **C** by the cause. Write **E** by the effect.

1. Emilio's family moved. _____

   Emilio missed his friends Carlos and John. _____

2. Emilio's sister was happy. _____

   She had the kitten she always wanted. _____

3. Emilio's mother was taking classes at the college. _____

   She was learning new things. _____

4. Emilio's father got a job at the TV station. _____

   He met celebrities. _____

5. Emilio decided to walk down to the creek. _____

   He wanted to see the tadpoles. _____

6. There was a drought. _____

   There was not much water in the creek. _____

7. The water was evaporating fast. _____

   The tadpoles would not have time to grow into frogs. _____

8. Emilio ran to the house to get a plastic jar. _____

   He wanted to save the tadpoles. _____

9. Read the cause. Write a possible effect.

   Cause: Emilio gave some of the tadpoles a safe place to live.

   Effect: _____

10. Write a sentence telling the main idea of the story.

   _____

   _____

☐ **I can use details to determine the theme of a text.**
☐ **I can read and comprehend grade-level fiction text.**

Name_____

Prize Pumpkin

Read the poem. Use context clues to infer the answers to the questions.

I went to the County Pumpkin Fest,
Hoping my pumpkin would be
judged best.
I lugged it all the way to the fair,
Huffing and puffing in crisp,
fresh air.
But, then I learned to my surprise,
That the judging was for pumpkin pies!

1. In what season does this poem take place? _____

    How do you know? _____

2. Do you think the writer won the prize? _____

    How do you know? _____

3. What size was the writer's pumpkin? _____

    How do you know? _____

4. What do you think happened next? _____

    _____

☐   **I can use details and examples in a text to explain and draw inferences.**
☐   **I can read and comprehend grade-level fiction text.**

Late-Night TV

Read the story. Use context clues to infer the answers to the questions.

Quinn woke up and heard strange sounds coming from the living room. She picked up her clock to check the time. It was very late!

Perplexed, she went to investigate. She discovered that the television was on—a late-night show was playing. Lying on the couch was a woman wearing a white coat. She was asleep.

Oh, Mom, Quinn thought. She must have worked late. She's always staying extra hours to help her sick patients get better.

Quinn turned off the TV. She tiptoed to Mom's side and eased her out of her white jacket. Mom did not even stir.

Quinn covered her up with an afghan and tiptoed back to bed. Soon, the whole house was quiet . . . except for the sound of snoring.

1. Is Quinn a boy or a girl? _____

   How do you know? _____

   _____

2. What does Mom do for a living? _____

   How do you know? _____

   _____

3. How does Quinn know that Mom is tired? _____

   _____

4. Does the story take place during the day or night? _____

   How do you know? _____

   _____

5. What does Quinn do at the very end of the story? _____

   How do you know? _____

   _____

☐ **I can use details and examples in a text to explain and draw inferences.**
☐ **I can read and comprehend grade-level fiction text.**

Sick Day

Look at the picture. Infer the answers to the questions.

"Hello, Ms. Prince? David won't be in today. I think he has a rash."

1. To whom is the mother talking? _____

    How do you know? _____

2. Is David really sick? _____

    How do you know? _____

3. What do you think will happen after David's mother discovers the paint? _____

    _____

    _____

☐   **I can use details and examples in a text to explain and draw inferences.**
☐   **I can use illustrations and other visuals to support what I know about a text.**

Name_____

Mystery of the Smudged Words

Read the story. Look at the message. Use context clues to infer the answers to the questions.

Amy came in from playing outside and opened a letter from her pen pal. Her fingers were sweaty, and some of the ink from the page got on her hands.

Amy peered closely at the letter. There were several smudges on it. Amy couldn't make out all of the words. She mentioned the problem to her mother.

"Mom," Amy said, "I can't figure out what these three words are. They're covered with a purple stain."

"Use the context to help you," Amy's mother suggested.

"What do you mean?" Amy inquired.

"The context includes the things surrounding what you are looking for," her mother said. "Look at the words around it. They will give you some clues."

"So, context clues are things that help you figure something out," Amy responded.

"Exactly!" her mother replied, beaming.

"I feel like a detective," Amy said proudly. "I'll try to solve the mystery of the purple-smudged words!"

Dear Amy,

Thanks for ~~smudge~~ me back so quickly! I enjoyed your letter. It's a sunny afternoon in Phoenix. I'm out on the deck of my swimming ~~smudge~~ getting a suntan. Soon, I'll go for a dip. But first, I'll finish this yummy peanut butter and ~~smudge~~ sandwich and wait a half-hour. Mom says I should wait after eating. Mothers! They sure have a lot of rules! Well, I hope to hear from you soon!

Yours truly,
Debbie

---

1. What is the first smudged word? _____

   What are the clues?_____

2. What is the second smudged word? _____

   What are the clues?_____

3. What is the third smudged word?_____

   What are the clues?_____

☐ **I can figure out the meaning of words and phrases in a text using context clues.**

☐ **I can read and comprehend grade-level fiction text.**

First School Day

Read the story. Answer the questions on page 81.

"Rise and shine, Gregory," Mrs. Roy said as she gazed down at the lump in the bed. "Today is a big day!"

The lump did not move. Mrs. Roy leaned over and shook the bed. A groan came from beneath the covers. Gregory rolled out from under them.

Mrs. Roy approached the second bed. "Wake up, Christopher! Summer is over. No more sleeping late." A head slowly peeked out, followed by the rest of a disheveled body.

"Be downstairs in 10 minutes," the boys' mother instructed. She left the room.

Gregory went into the bathroom and turned on the water. "Thith will be a thuper year," he said. A toothbrush extended from his mouth.

"What?" Christopher asked. He changed out of his pajamas and into blue jeans. He heard Gregory spit into the sink.

"I said 'this will be a super year,'" Gregory repeated. "New classes, new teachers, and a junior basketball team!" He winked.

Christopher looked a bit less confident. "I'm pretty nervous," he admitted. "I'm new at this, you know."

"Oh, middle school takes a little getting used to," Gregory agreed. "But, after a few days it will feel like you've been there forever! Remember, I had to go through it last year."

"Now, you're a *big* seventh grader and practically run the school," Christopher teased.

"Just don't do anything to ruin my reputation," Gregory warned, smiling back.

"You mean like tell everyone how you think Jenny Page is the prettiest girl in the school?"

Gregory blushed. Just then, some wonderful smells wafted into the room. Both boys halted and inhaled deeply.

"Race you downstairs!" Gregory shouted. The boys ran off to start the new year.

☐   I can read and comprehend grade-level fiction text.

First School Day (cont.)

Use context clues from the story on page 80 to infer answers to the questions.

1. How do the boys feel about waking up early?_____

   _____

2. What makes this a "big day"?_____

   _____

3. Describe the boys' relationship to each other. _____

   _____

4. At what time of day does this episode take place? _____

   _____

5. Why is Gregory difficult to understand when he first speaks?_____

   _____

6. What grade is Christopher entering? _____

7. How does each boy feel about the upcoming year?

   Gregory: _____

   _____

   Christopher: _____

   _____

8. What is waiting for the boys downstairs? _____

☐   I can use details and examples in a text to explain and draw inferences.

The Big Concert

Look at the illustrations. Infer what is happening. Write a sentence to describe what the girl wants in each frame.

Example: Frame 1

The girl wants <u>to go to the concert</u>.

1. Frame 2

   The girl wants _____ .

2. Frame 3

   The girl wants _____ .

3. Frames 4 and 5

   The girl wants _____ .

☐   I can use details and examples in a text to explain and draw inferences.
☐   I can make connections between text and a visual.
☐   I can use illustrations and other visuals to support what I know about a text.

82

Bad Air Blues

Read the story. Answer the questions on page 84.

The alarm clock blared its disturbingly cheerful tune. Chase Foster groaned as he pried open his eyelids—and wheezed. He reached for the inhaler on the nightstand and took a puff. Chase sighed as he rose and padded to the living room.

"How are you feeling this morning?" his mother asked. "Are you having trouble breathing?"

"I feel terrific, Mom. I've never felt better."

His mother looked doubtful. "Tonight's soccer game has been canceled due to poor air quality."

"Are you sure?"

She nodded. "This drought has lasted for weeks, and there isn't the slightest breeze to blow the pollution away."

Winsome Valley was a great place to live. Citizens looked out for one another, businesses thrived, and the population grew at a steady but manageable rate. No community was finer—unless it did not rain.

Without precipitation or a good breeze to keep them from settling, particulates hovered over Winsome Valley like a sallow, greasy fog. Dust, pollen, smoke, and car exhaust blanketed the valley. Healthy people experienced stinging eyes and coughs. People with illnesses like asthma faced serious breathing problems.

"What does the weather forecast predict?" asked Chase.

His mother stroked his hair and smiled. "Your heart is set on this camping trip, isn't it?"

"We're going to go canoeing and horseback riding. It's our last chance before school starts." Chase gave his mother his saddest expression.

"You can't go if the air quality is bad, Chase."

Chase sighed. He felt disappointed because he was so excited to camp.

She must have noticed because she patted his shoulder and said in a sympathetic tone, "Weather is changeable, Chase. Don't give up hope. All we need is a little rain or a steady breeze. On Friday, you should be heading to Winsome Valley State Park."

☐ **I can read and comprehend grade-level fiction text.**

Bad Air Blues (cont.)

Use context clues from the story on page 83 and this weather forecast to answer the questions.

National Weather Service Five-Day Forecast for Winsome Valley

Wednesday	**Thursday**	**Friday**	**Saturday**	**Sunday**
Chance of rain: 80%	Chance of Rain: 90%	Chance of rain: 60%	Chance of rain: 40%	Chance of rain: 40%
Mild winds from the north	Strong winds from the north	Mild winds from the north	Mild winds from the east	Breezy winds from the east

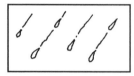 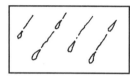   

1. What condition does Chase have?

    a. He has a cold.

    b. He has asthma.

    c. He has a sprained ankle.

2. If the weather forecast is accurate, will Chase go camping? _____

    How do you know?_____

3. Write an ending for the story.

    _____

    _____

    _____

    _____

☐   I can use details and examples in a text to explain and draw inferences.
☐   I can use illustrations and other visuals to support what I know about a text.

To the Moon!

Read the paragraph. Use context clues to infer the meaning of the words in boldface. Circle the correct answers to the questions.

When astronauts explored the moon in the late 1960s and early 1970s, they collected samples of moon rocks for scientists to study. It was difficult to **trek** across the rough **lunar** surface. It was even hard to **haul** all of the samples back to the lunar module, not because they were heavy, but because they were **bulky**. The astronauts needed some kind of vehicle. NASA invented a car for them. It was called the Lunar **Rover** or moon buggy.

1. The word *trek* means
   a. ride.
   b. hike.
   c. dance.

2. The word *lunar* relates to
   a. the stars.
   b. the sun.
   c. the moon.

3. The word *haul* means
   a. walk.
   b. carry.
   c. play.

4. The word *rover* means
   a. traveler.
   b. builder.
   c. worker.

5. The word *bulky* means
   a. tiny
   b. blue.
   c. large.

6. Fill in the missing word. Smooth is to rough as bulky is to _____ .

   large   carry   compact

☐   I can use details and examples in a text to explain and draw inferences.
☐   I can figure out the meaning of words or phrases in informational text.

Final Exam

Mrs. Lindsey's class had their final exam on Monday. Not everyone studied for it, though. Look at the pictures. Use context clues to infer the answers to the questions.

1. On Sunday, the boy _____ .   studied   did not study

    When the test was given on Monday, he felt _____   confident   nervous

    because he was _____ .   prepared   not prepared

2. What grade do you think he received? _____

3. On Sunday, the girl _____ .   studied   did not study

    When the test was given on Monday, she felt _____   alert   sleepy

    because she was _____ .   rested   not rested

4. What grade do you think she received? _____

❑ **I can use details and examples in a text to explain and draw inferences.**
❑ **I can make connections between text and a visual.**

Word Clues

Read the clues. Infer the name of the object the clues describe. Write the name on the line.

1. Some people collect me.

   People stick me on packages.

   Without me, you wouldn't receive your birthday cards in the mail!

   I am a _____ .

2. Objects made of metal cling to me.

   I have a north pole and a south pole.

   I can stick to refrigerators.

   I am a _____ .

3. I am a narrow, flexible strip.

   I protect wounds from bacteria.

   I stick to skin but not cuts.

   I am an _____ .

4. I am a ball of hot gas.

   Astronomers study me.

   I burn brightly in the sky.

   I am a _____ .

5. I am a source of bright light.

   You often use me indoors.

   I come in different types, such as CFL or fluorescent.

   I am a _____ .

6. I am a bright flash of light in the sky.

   You'll sometimes see me when it's wet outside.

   Thunder usually follows me.

   I am _____ .

- ☐ **I can use details and examples in a text to explain and draw inferences.**
- ☐ **I can read and comprehend grade-level fiction text.**

Name_____

Most Valuable Player

Read the story and look at the picture. Identify how Mona feels. Write a letter to a friend with clues that help your friend infer how Mona feels.

Mona had sweaty hands as she gripped the bat. This was the last inning of the game, and the score was still tied. She stepped up to the plate and waited for the pitcher to throw the ball.

The ball came fast. Mona swung. She hit the ball so hard it flew into the air and over the fence. A home run!

Dear _____ ,

_____

_____

_____

_____

_____

_____

_____

_____

_____

_____

What are the context clues in your letter?

1. _____

2. _____

3. _____

☐   I can use details and examples in a text to explain and draw inferences.

☐   I can read and comprehend grade-level fiction text.

Save the Day

Read the story. Answers the questions on page 90.

Tate raced toward the baseball diamond. He greeted his teammates, jumping up and down. "Are you ready to win the championship?" he asked.

His two best friends, Jeffrey and Amira, smiled at his excitement. "It looks like our star batter is ready," Jeffrey said.

Jeffrey did not want to admit that he was nervous. Lately, he had been in a slump. His average had declined late in the season. He hoped he could pull it back up today when it counted most.

Amira was calm, as usual. She never seemed to get butterflies in her stomach, even under pressure. She was the team's pitcher and had a mean fastball.

The players warmed up and took the field. The game was a close one, but Tate and his team were victorious in the end. Afterward, the three buddies went to an ice cream shop to celebrate.

"Great job today, Amira!" Tate complimented his friend. "You kept your cool even when we were behind two to zero."

"Thanks." Amira said. She licked at her black raspberry ice cream. Not a drip escaped off the cone.

"You were great too!" Tate said to Jeffrey. "When you hit that ball over the fence in the fifth inning, I almost knocked the bench over while cheering!"

The two boys gave each other high fives. In their enthusiasm, the boys knocked Tate's ice cream off its cone.

"Oh, no," Tate said.

"Sorry, Tate," Jeffrey said. But, Jeffrey could not stop smiling. He was in too good a mood. He'd hit the winning run today, and he felt great. He hadn't let his team down. Now, he would not let his friend down.

"I have some money left," he said to Tate. "Let's go back up to the counter, so I can save the day again!"

❏ **I can read and comprehend grade-level fiction text.**

Save the Day (cont.)

Use context clues from the story on page 89 to answer the questions.

1. How does Tate feel before the game? _____

   How do you know?_____

   _____

2. Do you think Tate played well in the game? _____

   How do you know?_____

   _____

3. How does Jeffrey feel before the game? _____

   How do you know?_____

   _____

4. Do you think Jeffrey played well in the game? _____

   How do you know?_____

   _____

5. How does Amira feel before the game? _____

   How do you know?_____

   _____

6. Do you think Amira played well in the game? _____

   How do you know?_____

   _____

❑ I can use details and examples in a text to explain and draw inferences.
❑ I can summarize the text.

Name_____

Inferring

A Very Rainy Day

Read the story. Use context clues to infer the answers to the questions.

The wind had finally died down, and the rain had stopped. Paige and her parents were sitting in the living room of their house, which was dark except for a single candle's light.

"Let's find out what's going on outside," Paige's mom suggested as she turned on the small radio.

"...has moved out of the area," an announcer's voice boomed. "Winds reaching nearly 100 miles an hour passed through our town this morning. But, the worst is over, and it is now safe to go outside." Suddenly, the radio went dead. The house was quiet again.

"Well," Paige's dad said optimistically, "at least we heard some good news, even if it was cut short. Let's look out the window and survey the damage."

Paige raced to the window and peered outside. She saw tree branches strewn across the lawn. The mailbox was bent at a crazy angle, and some of the letters and numbers of their address on the mailbox were missing.

"The wind must have blown them off," Paige's father noted. As he read the remaining letters he began to chuckle. Paige and her mom joined in the mirth.

The mailbox displayed

_____ _____R _____ AIN.

1. The weather event that took place that day was _____ .

2. The living room was dark because the storm had _____ .

3. The power source for the radio they were using was _____ .

4. After the storm had passed, the family felt _____ .

5. The family's name could have been

      a. Main.   b. Crain.   c. Germain.

☐ I can use details and examples in a text to explain and draw inferences.
☐ I can read and comprehend grade-level fiction text.

© Carson-Dellosa • CD-104661

Answer Key

Page 12
Circle: 1. science fiction;
2. poetry; 3. historical fiction;
4. biography; 5. folktale; Write:
6: fairy tale; 7. science fiction;
8. biography; 9. fantasy;
10. poetry

Page 13
Circle: 1. science fiction;
2. fantasy; 3. historical fiction;
4. realistic fiction

Page 14
1. biography; 2. tall tale; 3.
science fiction; 4. realistic
fiction; 5. myth; 6. tall tale

Page 15
1. f; 2. d; 3. b; 4. a; 5. c; 6. e; 7.
i; 8. h; 9. j; 10. k; 11. l; 12. g; 13–18.
Answers will vary.

Page 16
1. R; 2. R; 3. F; 4. R; 5. R; 6. F; 7. F;
8. R; 9. R; 10. F

Page 17
1. b; 2. e; 3. i; 4. a; 5. f; 6. h;
7. d; 8. j; 9. c; 10. g

Page 18
1. g; 2. a; 3. d; 4. c; 5. h; 6. b;
7. e; 8. f

Page 19
1. Ned Tuttle; 2. Dorothy Wells;
3. Lonnie Lorenzo; 4. Helene;
5. Dora the deer mouse;
6. Lady Beatrice; 7. Steven

Page 20
1. b; 2. d; 3. e; 4. a; 5. c;
6–10. Answers will vary.

Page 21
1. Cal's bedroom; 2. Cal and
Cleo, twin brother and sister;
3. They need money to go to
an amusement park. 4. They
decide to rake their neighbors'
leaves to earn money.

Page 23
1. summer; camp; 2. see baby
possums/in crook of the
beech tree/second day, sing
songs/in dining hall/ every
noon, discover blue racer/
in field/fifth day, sketch plant
specimens/in a national park/
drizzly day, hear silly stories/
in cabin/bedtime, observe
raccoons/in woods/one night;
3. Answers will vary but may
include campers live in cabins,
they visit a national park for
nature hikes, and there is a
lake and a large dining hall.

Page 24
1. a. Monday afternoon,
classroom; b. September 25,
Dilly Pond; c. 30 years later,
school laboratory; 2. He is a
science teacher. 3. It helped
him know what he wanted to
do with his life. 4. Answers
will vary.

Page 25
1. one summer night, on a
beach; 2. on an autumn
morning, in a big yard; 3. on a
wintry day, in a snowy field;
4. early spring, in a garden;
5. during baseball season, on
a baseball field

Page 27
1. a. 7; b. 10; c. 8; d. 12; 2.
a. Bandhavgarh National Park;
b. Taj Majal; c. Bandhavgarh
National Park; d. Ladakh or
Zaskar Mountains; e. Thar
Desert; 3–5. Answers will vary.

Page 28
1. b; 2. c; 3. a

Page 29
1. insects, chemicals, light, mate,
hatch, adults; 2–3. Answers will
vary.

Page 30
1. b; 2. a; 3. c; 4. d

Page 31
1. f; 2. b; 3. d; 4. e; 5. a; 6. c

Page 32
1. A child plants a tree to
help him deal with missing
a grandparent. 2. his
grandparent's love; 3. the
beauty of the world and
love; 4. anchored; 5. Answers
will vary but may include
celebrate the beauty, loving
embrace, and life.

Page 33
1. c; 2. a; 3 Answers will vary
but may include the dog
loves the food she gets, the
petting, the playing, and her
owner talks to her. 4. Answers
will vary but may include that
from the dog's point of view,
her owner will love and care
for her no matter what.

Answer Key

Page 34

Answers will vary but should include each underlined word from the passage.

Page 35

1. Light travels into the eye where the lens focuses it. It is then projected onto the retina, which sends this message (image) to the brain. 2. One sees at 20 feet what a person with normal vision sees at 80 feet. 3. One sees at 40 feet what a person with normal vision can only see at 20 feet. 4. Answers will vary.

Page 36

1. Charles Conrad, Jr. was an active participant in the United States space program. 2. 1962; 3. 1969; 4. 21; 5. *Gemini;* 6. sequentially or in an outline; 7. Answers will vary.

Page 37

1. Answers will vary but may include that he was a doctor of science with an interest in medicine. 2. pasteurization; 3. He developed pasteurization. 4. His work was widely known and he was often spoke at international medical meetings.

Page 38

1. a; 2. b; 3. pushing a swing by holding the seat with both hands and running forward and under the swing seat; 4. Answers will vary.

Page 39

Answers will vary but each two-sentence summary should include detail-supporting words from the text.

Page 40

1. C; 2. A; 3. D; 4. B; 5. A; 6. D; 7. C; 8. B; 9. C; 10. B; 11. A; 12. D; 13. B; 14. D

Page 41

1. Answers will vary but may include: I. native people of western United States; II. once traveled with the seasons; III. live on reservations today; IV. believed in a creator god; V. Sacagawea was a Shoshoni woman; VI. She helped Lewis and Clark. 2. Answers will vary but may include that it helps to condense and keep track of large amounts of information.

Page 42

1. Answers will vary but may include: The lunches of the narrator keep disappearing from the refrigerator. After a week, Mom steps in to figure out which of the five brothers is taking the lunch. Mom decides to ask Dad's advice. During dinner, Dad admits that he is the one taking the lunches. 2. Answers will vary but may include Dad thought the lunch was for him since it was the only one in the refrigerator. The narrator could not understand who would take the lunch. 3. Answers will vary but may include: The narrator is a girl. The brothers are mentioned as a group several times. The narrator appears to feel differently from them.

Page 43

1. c; 2. a. The package arrived late. b. The audio was not good. c. The game froze up. d. The game caused meltdown of gaming system.

Page 44

Answers will vary but may include: A: 1. House has three windows. 2. There is one planet in the sky. 3. Father has a mustache. 4. Father has a newspaper. 5. Dog has one eye. 6. Kid has plain shirt. 7. Ball has swirled design. 8. Car has two lights. 9. Scooter has no headlight. 10. Door has round window. B. 1. House has two windows. 2. Two planets are in sky; 3. Father is clean-shaven. 4. Father has a magazine. 5. Dog has two eyes. 6. Kid has striped shirt. 7. Ball has zigzags. 8. Car has three lights. 9. Scooter has headlight. 10. Door has triangular window.

Page 45

1. bark; 2. glass/cup; 3. fur; 4. paint; 5 wet; 6. field/stadium; 7. air/helium. 8. D. 9. plane; 10. bee, bird

Answer Key

Page 46
1. b; 2. c; 3. a; 4. a; 5. b; 6. c; 7. b

Page 47
2. b; 3. c. 4. a; 5. d;
6. encyclopedia, atlas;
7. dictionary, thesaurus

Page 48
1. horse; 2. pyramid; 3. Danny;
4. disappointed; 5. neighbor;
6. married; 7. jeans; Circled:
8. c; 9. a; 10. c; 11. b; 12. a; 13. a

Page 49
1. *The Magic Baseball*; 2. *Dance until You Drop*; 3. *Olden Days*;
4. *Adventures of Mama Llama*;
5. *Together Forever*

Page 50
1. c; 2. c; 3. c; 4. b; 5. b; 6. c;
7. b; 8. a

Page 51
1. b; 2. b; 3. a; 4. c; 5. d; 6. d;
7. c; 8. b; 9. a; 10. c;
11. Answers will vary.

Page 53
1. Daniel; Answers will vary but may include: a. He saw the knife first. b. He noticed the footprints. c. He saw the footprint on the step. 2. b. The person had not used it yet. c. The person was young and/or small. d. The person was inside the shed. Check students' starring and circling. 3. a. Nancy; b. Answers will vary but may include Nancy is

described as little, she makes a mess, and she does not realize she has caused a problem.
4. a. Kay. b. Answers will vary but may include Kay seems to be in charge, Daniel asks her opinion, and Kay takes care of Nancy.

Page 54
1. Jake; 2. Jessica; 3. Julia;
4. Josh; 5. Jordan; 6. Josh;
7. Jake; 8. Julia, Jessica;
9. Jessica; 10. Jake; 11. Jessica, Jordan

Page 55
B, P, B; Answers will vary.

Page 56
1. a. solid; b. liquid; c. gas;
2. faster; 3. gas; 4. shape;
5. does not have definite shape; 6. cannot be easily changed; 7. does not have a definite shape or volume;
8. yes; 9. Answers will vary.
10. no; 11. yes; 12. Answers will vary. 13. no; 14. Answers will vary. 15. Answers will vary but may include an encyclopedia.
16. Answers will vary but may include *solid*, *liquid*, *gas*, or *matter*.

Page 57
1. lake or canal; 2. bicycle; 3. oink; 4. bat; 5. cake; 6. puppy;
7. train; 8. Chinese; 9. lion;
10. shoe or sock; 11. zipper;
12. end or finish; 13. night;
14–15. Pictures should reflect the analogy.

Page 58
1. opinion; 2. opinion; 3. fact;
4. opinion; 5. fact; 6. fact;
7. opinion; 8. fact; 9. fact;
10–11. Answers will vary.

Page 59
1. N; 2. S; 3. N; 4. N; 5. S; 6. N;
7. S; 8. S; 9. Answers will vary but may include individual states could keep more control over issues.
10. Answers will vary.

Page 60
1. a; 2. c; 3. b; 4. a; 5. a

Page 61
1. a, b, d; 2. c, e, f

Page 62
1. c; 2. d; 3. a; 4. b

Page 63
1. d; 2. a; 3. b; 4. c

Page 64
1. b; 2. d; 3. a; 4. c

Page 65
Calvin stayed in his house: g, i, j; We traded in our old car: b, d, e; The snake crawled into the hole: c, h, l; We played soccer: a, f, k

Page 66
Underline: 1. Omar stubbed his toe; 2. The rain was coming into the house; 3. I was full from the tasty chicken soup;
4. she missed an easy layup;
5. we mixed vinegar and baking soda; 6. he was excited

Answer Key

to fly for the first time; 7. the theater lights were turned on; 8. he is interested in modern art; 9. she had no kings; Circle: 1. he cried out, "Ouch!" 2. we shut the windows; 3. I slept like a baby; 4. Karen was disappointed; 5. It erupted; 6. David could not sit still; 7. I was blinded for a moment; 8. Ted begged to see the newest art exhibit; 9. Tanya said, "Go fish!"

Page 67
1. He went to the beach. 2. He went shopping. 3. He saw a movie. 4. He was late to school. 5. He took too long in the bathroom. 6. He got an A+ on the assignment.

Page 68
Underline: 1. President Jefferson was interested in finding a water route for trade to the Pacific Ocean; 2. her husband Toussaint Charbonneau was hired as a guide; 3. she was Shoshone; 4. he was only a baby; 5. To move the expedition's freight upriver; 6. Because of her herbal knowledge; 7. she met her older brother, now a chief among her people; 8. her husband was officially hired by the expedition and she was not; 9. There are conflicting reports about Sacagawea's later life; Circle: 1. he

commissioned an expedition; 2. Sacagawea joined the Corps of Discovery; 3. Sacagawea could help Lewis and Clark's expeditionary force obtain food and supplies from her people; 4. Sacagawea carried her son on her back; 5. the group hired a large keelboat; 6. Sacagawea's tasks included gathering edible plants; 7. The young woman was surprised; 8. Sacagawea received no personal compensation; 9. historians consider her a puzzle; 10. b

Page 69
Answers will vary but may include: 1. you have a sprained ankle or sore back. 2. you need a hot pack. 3. you need a cold pack. 4. break the water pouch inside. 5. Completely mix the water with the chemicals. 6. Hot and cold pouches use a chemical reaction to create instant heat or cold.

Page 70
Answers will vary but may include: 1. She ate her food. She had yet to pack her lunch. 2. It was a school holiday. He already finished his homework. 3. He was catching the flu. He ate something unpleasant. 4. It was raining. The dog went swimming. 5. The oven was too hot. We

left it in for too long. 6. It liked howling at the moon. It was scared of a man nearby. 7. Stories will vary but should include one of the cause and effects on the page.

Page 71
Answers will vary but may include: 1. He blew up the balloon. 2. She fell off her bike. 3. It was a snow day. 4. I won the race. 5. Answers will vary but could include: I discovered hair gel tastes terrible. 6. Dani shared the burger with her dog.

Page 72
1. Flowering plants are vital to bees. 2. Bees are diverse insects. 3. Bee colonies are complex. 4. Farmers depend on bees. 5. Answers will vary.

Page 73
1. The bus had a flat tire. 2. Josh needed help. 3. It had slipped under his dresser. 4. He hoped to find his grandfather's watch. 5. He had the address. 6. It was their first case in a long time. 7. They were late. 8. The house had a messy yard. 9. The dresser was in Josh's room. 10. Dylan looked under the dresser. 11. Answers will vary but may include: The Mystery Society solved the mystery of the missing watch.

Answer Key

Page 74

Causes: 1. a. mowing lawns; b. saved his earnings; 2. a. forgot to water The plant; b. Becca watered it; 3. a. having studied very hard; b. Carla made a perfect score on the test; Effects: 1. a. earned money; b. he could afford to buy a new bike; 2. a. the plant wilted; b. the plant became healthy; 3. a. Carla finished the test easily; b. brought her grade to an A; Inferences: Answers will vary but may include: 1. Andre was determined. 2. Becca was forgetful. 3. Carla is studious.

Page 75

1. C, E; 2. E, C; 3. C, E; 4. C, E; 5. E, C; 6. C, E; 7. C, E; 8. E, C; 9. Answers will vary but may include the tadpoles grew into frogs. 10. Answers will vary but may include Emilio's family moved.

Page 76

1. autumn; Pumpkins are an autumn vegetable. 2. no; He did not have a pie. 3. large; The speaker huffed while lugging it. 4. Answers will vary.

Page 77

1. girl; Quinn is called "she." 2. doctor; She worked late to help sick patients and wears a white coat. 3. Mom fell asleep on the couch. 4. night; It is very late. 5. She goes back to sleep. The house is full of snores.

Page 78

Answers will vary but may include: 1. the teacher or school nurse; She must call the school for a sick day. 2. no; He painted on the spots and is hiding the paintbrush behind his back. 3. Answers will vary.

Page 79

1. writing; Debbie is thanking her for her letter. 2. pool; Debbie is lying on the deck and going to take a dip. 3. jelly; It goes with peanut butter in a sandwich.

Page 81

1. They do not like it. 2. It is the first day of school. 3. They are brothers. 4. morning; 5. He is brushing his teeth. 6. sixth; 7. Gregory: excited, Christopher: nervous; 8. breakfast

Page 82

Answers will vary but may include: 1. to earn money for tickets; 2. to buy a ticket with the money she earned; 3. to meet the musicians and get an autograph

Page 84

1. b; 2. yes; It will rain and the wind will blow the dust away. 3. Answers will vary.

Page 85

1. b; 2. c; 3. b; 4. a; 5. c; 6. compact

Page 86

1. studied, confident, prepared; 2. A; 3. did not study, sleepy, not rested; 4. a bad grade

Page 87

1. stamp; 2. magnet; 3. adhesive bandage; 4. star; 5. lightbulb; 6. lightning

Page 88

Letters will vary. 1–3. Answers will vary but should show context from the letter.

Page 90

1. excited and confident; He jumps up and down. 2. probably; He was the star batter. 3. nervous; His batting average has gone down. 4. yes; He hit the winning home run. 5. relaxed and calm; She never gets butterflies in her stomach. 6. yes; She kept her cool even when they were losing.

Page 91

1. a hurricane; 2. knocked out the electricity; 3. batteries; 4. relieved; 5. c